How to Hypnotise
Stage, Street and Therapy
By Steve Leap

This book is dedicated to my entire family . Thanks for putting up with me. Also thanks goes out to all the barista's at
Neros coffee shop in Boston Lincs England

FORWARD

I have been an avid student of hypnosis in its varied forms for over twenty years. I say student because the subject matter is so deep (no pun intended) that I believe it can never be fully understood let alone mastered. The term practitioner implies that one knows everything there is to know. In my humble opinion this can never be the case. There is always something new to embrace. In fact if there weren't then there would be no knew literature or workshops etc, and there are plenty out there.

Anyone who has any understanding of hypnosis will tell you that not only are they learning new procedures, scripts etc every day, but they are also finding new twists on existing ones. Also every subject/ volunteer/ victim you come across is different and needs treating as an individual this in fact itself should be proof enough.

Anyone can learn a couple of inductions and read from scripts in a therapy room or indeed copy someone else's comedy routine for a stage show. And many do. I have witnessed dozens of second rate comedy hypnosis performers doing just that. The only thing that sets them apart from any 'ordinary' person is the confidence it takes to get up in front of an audience. More about confidence later.

Real professionals learn the craft inside and out then go on to create their own material be it for stage, the therapy room or even for covert or street hypnosis. Granted for the beginner using tried and tested methods from others is probably the way to go initially. However as soon as you are confident and competent you should be writing your own material and then modifying it on a patient to patient basis.

Most books are written either for the therapist and are overly serious, or for the stage performer and these can be a little too light hearted. Other books covering covert hypnosis or NLP or a mixture of both, seem to be written for the real power freaks who want to mind control others. If mind control is your motive for reading this or any other book, don't bother. You cannot control the mind of another person full stop.

You will find this book has not been written like most hypnosis books. In this book you will find each section is devoted to all three. For example under the heading inductions you will find the relative information for stage, therapy and street.

CONTENTS

INTRODUCTION

This book is for anyone wishing to use hypnotism without any prior knowledge. In it all aspects are dealt with from the therapy room through stage all the way to street hypnosis.

The contents are set out similar to my hypnosis course. Read the entire book first then go on to carry out the exercises in the last chapter and you won't go far wrong.

Included are samples of various types of inductions. There are no detailed scripts since in honesty this is a subject matter in itself. For more inductions scripts etc look out for my other books on hypnosis as you become more skilled you will need to pick those up as well. Also there is my A to Z of hypnotic terms, this will be an invaluable reference tool for both the beginner and accomplished hypnotist. As you will gather from reading this book I believe that to be great in the hypnotic world you will need to be a good all round mentalist.

Mentalists combine the art of hypnosis, cold reading and non verbal reading as well as a bit of good old fashioned magic. If you can master these you will be truly awesome in your chosen path.

Happy reading

CHAPTER ~ 1 ~ THE BASICS

Parts of the mind

The mind, as we call it is such a complex system that we will probably never truly understand it. Most of the literature on the mind and hypnosis claims that there is two parts of the mind. The conscious and the subconscious as well as something called the critical factor.

I believe there is only one mind but within it there are four distinct functions. These four parts interact, overlap and consult each other all of the time.

There are the things we do unconsciously such as breathing and non verbal communication (unconscious)

There are things we do subconsciously like store memories, habits use our imagination etc.(subconscious)

There are things we do consciously like writing or reading. (conscious)

Then there is the attention or focus this is our thinking mind, our gate keeper. (thought)

The analogy I like to use is of a computer and its operator, since these days most people have at least a rudimentary understanding of these complex machines and it is easy to compare a computer to a brain.

The unconscious. (Breathing)

Background activity such as refreshing the screen constantly or running the internal clock.

The subconscious. (memories, habits, emotions and imagination)

This is akin to the Hard Drive, It stores all the data which we have 'saved' like documents or preset responses.

The conscious. (writing)

Interpreting input, this is like the computer turning zeros and ones into letters that have been typed into the keyboard

Attention/ Focus. (gatekeeper)

Consider the gatekeeper to be a bit like a spellchecker.

Before we can have an understanding of what hypnosis is we need to understand how these four parts interact with each other. Then we can know what is required to hypnotise someone, instead of thinking we are putting them to sleep and commanding their movements.

So we start with the background activity (unconscious), this carries on regardless doing the mundane things it needs to do for us to exist and interaction with it is negligible. So the internal clock just ticks away no matter what the circumstances. Then an operator sits at the keyboard and starts typing and the keys on the keyboard turn the input into letters on the screen (conscious) at the same time the spellchecker (attention) is running its eye over the inputs it constantly consults the information stored in the Hard drive (subconscious) and either leaves the letters on the screen as they are or underlines them as incorrect.

So you see no matter the keyboard input, the Hard Drive, through the gatekeeper will always win. It wins because the information it has just 'IS'. This is true of our minds Hard Drive too, information in the subconscious just is, If there is ever a conflict between the conscious and the subconscious the subconscious will always win. If you are using a computer and you type the UK version of colour, and the settings are for the US the word will be highlighted as incorrect. A human example of this is someone wanting to stop smoking they consciously try and try but the subconscious just keeps saying 'I'm a smoker' light one up!

We can change the results from the spellchecker. But in order to do this we need to change the Information in the Hard Drive. To do this we need to distract the spellchecker for a moment keep it focused on doing nothing in particular. To do this we open the spellchecker option box, whilst it is open the spell checker is just sort of hanging around focusing on keeping the option box open. Then we select the option to allow the word, such as the differently spelt colour, then 'save or add to dictionary' in the Hard Drive. Presto next time we type 'colour' it is accepted as a correct spelling. This in essence is what we do in hypnosis. We keep the conscious in limbo, the gatekeepers attention focused elsewhere and communicate with the subconscious.

When we add a few more ingredients to the pot we can see why hypnosis is such a powerful tool. And why people are prone to do the stupidest thing whilst taking part in a stage show.

The conscious activity is logical, analytical.

The gatekeeper is a go between and refers to the subconscious for truth, habit, memory.

The subconscious activity is illogical, imagination and creativity lives here.

So let's put it all together and look at what happens to a suggestion given to a subject in a comedy stage setting.

Firstly I suggest to an un-hypnotised person that they are the world's greatest guitar player and that they have an imaginary guitar and that when they hear a particular piece of music they will stand up and give the performance of their life.

The conscious hears the suggestion the gatekeeper focuses on it momentarily, asks the opinion of the subconscious. The subconscious searches the memory banks and replies. 'no we are not the world's greatest guitar player' and that's the end of it there is no reaction.

Now I make the same suggestion to a hypnotised person. The conscious is in limbo and although it can hear the suggestion it doesn't really care since it is in limbo. The gatekeeper is focused on something else and even if it hears cannot be bothered to do its job. So the suggestion goes straight to the subconscious, remember what is in the subconscious simply 'IS'. PRESTO the hypnotised person behaves as if they are the best guitar player in the world giving his finest performance.

Imagination will always win in a contest with logic.

Uses for hypnosis

Therapy

This is when we use hypnosis to help a subject make a change to something unhealthy about themselves in order to make positive and permanent changes to their lives. This can be anything from becoming a non smoker, ridding themselves of a phobia, in fact just about anything. There are fundamentally two types of therapy open to use with hypnotism.

Direct suggestion therapy.

Changes are made by making and repeating suggestions to the subconscious that the desired change will happen. The suggestions must be repeated again and again since what is really being done is changing one habit for another and as we know habits take time to form. A rule of thumb to use is that the suggestion should be repeated about 15 times. Direct suggestion does not take into account that the phobia is a symptom or reaction to an event. If we remove the symptom using this technique then symptom replacement is likely to occur.

E.G. Using direct suggestion to rid the subjects fear of spiders. We would effectively tell the person not to be frightened of spiders. Of course it is a bit more complicated than that and we will cover it in depth later.

Analytical therapy.

Referring to the 'exercise caution' quote above analytical therapy means what it says. Analysing or finding out the root of an issue. When I say issue I mean a symptom. A symptom is a habit or reaction which a subject has as a means of protecting themselves. The subject has had an experience so traumatic that the conscious mind refuses to accept it. It is forced deep inside the subconscious. They either suppress or repress the memory but when confronted with similar situations the symptom shows itself. If a symptom is dealt with by using direct suggestion therapy the repression may still exist and will cause a different symptom. Imagine a client came to you because every time they saw a spider they sweat and scream, after 'curing' this phobia the client develops another symptom like coming out in a rash! Direct suggestion should only be used for reinforcing type therapies. Such as confidence building or self esteem issues.

I believe that in therapy it is always preferable to use the analytical approach since it is widely accepted that everything has a beginning. If we can find the beginning and change the reaction then we have succeeded.

E.G using analytical therapy to rid the fear of spiders we would regress them back to the time of the incident which triggered the emotional response the first time and then work to help them understand it better and reassure them. Again this will be covered in depth later.

Stage/street

This is when hypnosis is used to effectively create a temporary altered state or reality for the subject, usually for comic value. Volunteers or victims, depending on the situation, are made to experience all sorts of weird and wonderful things. They perform feats which under usual waking conditions they would not.

E.G. the best guitarist in the world scenario previously described.

Covert

Covert hypnosis is it seems the latest craze. Rooted firmly in NLP (Neuro -linguistic Programming). It uses subliminal messaging to persuade people, usually the unsuspecting, to do as they are instructed without even knowing that hypnotism has been used. We use covert hypnosis to embed new realities. Exactly like subliminal messaging used in advertising.

Unlike hypnosis for therapy or stage permission by the subject is not sought. The reason agreement is not usually obtained by the hypnotist is because it is he and not the subject who is likely to gain from the experience.

The exception for this is when covert hypnosis is used for entertainment. Perhaps to give the appearance that the hypnotist has magical powers such as mind reading abilities. There is usually an audience and it is done with an air of comedy.

For those thinking of using covert hypnosis for personal gain only to the detriment of others a word of warning. Hypnotists have been prosecuted and have served prison sentences. For they are indeed crimes. Taking a persons wallet from them using these techniques is entertaining but always give it back!

As a footnote to these brief explanations of how hypnosis is used it is worth mentioning, a constantly repeated, so called fact. That is people will not do anything under hypnosis which is against their basic principles or beliefs! You can form your own opinion on this matter however I believe this is not strictly true.

A person in a highly suggestible state may do just about anything if the suggestion is framed properly. So be very careful of the language you use

You have a subject in deep hypnosis and decide to tell them to cause some bodily harm to someone in the next room. Obviously for most people this would be against their principles and so the command would not be carried out. In fact it is likely that they would automatically terminate the trance and emerge from hypnosis. Unless of course they have criminal tendencies and are predisposed to this type of behaviour anyway.

Now take a person in deep hypnosis and tell their subconscious that they are a youngster taking part in a game and that in the next room is a dummy sitting on a chair and that to win the game the dummy must be destroyed etc... I'm sure you get the idea. If you appealed to the imagination enough and framed the suggestion correctly it might not be a lot different than the guitarist scenario yet again!

Stages and depths of hypnosis

It is generally purported that there are five stages to the hypnosis experience.

Waking

Light hypnosis

Medium hypnosis

Deep hypnosis

Somnambulistic

I prefer to use the following terms when describing hypnotic stages:

Awake

Light Trance

Medium Trance

Deep Trance

Hyper Trance

In the same breath it is also said that depth of relaxation is limitless. These statements are almost contradictory. I believe that we should look at the two together on a sort of sliding scale. Say from 1 to 100. 1 being the waking state and 100 being the deepest state, and that there is a smooth transition up and down the scale.

It is much more realistic to imagine steadily descending or ascending a long graduated scale instead of the implication that we drop off one step to another in five abrupt stages.

The five stages can still be used to punctuate the scale. For example you may describe a person as being in a light trance when they are in the first section of the scale 1-20. In the same way you might describe a hyper-trance state anywhere between 80 and 100.

It's easy to see that even in hyper-trance there is a variation of depth from one person to another, indeed for one experience to the other for the same subject. Also it is good from the point of view of the subjects understanding of their own experience. This will be explained in more depth when we discuss deepeners and depth tests.

Subjects understand this a lot easier especially if when doing a pre-talk we describe say 1 to 10 as being similar to daydreaming rather than the usual explanation of being in trance is like daydreaming which may conjure up all sorts of misconceptions. You could even see the scale as being from 1 to 1,000 it really doesn't matter. As long as the subject and the hypnotist understand that the stages of hypnosis is not so tightly organised as one to five.

It is also worth mentioning that every time a subject re-enters trance they become more suggestible so by definition it could be said they go into a deeper state. This is the basis of fractionation.

Identifying trance

Subjects in trance display many different traits. Remember everyone is different so don't go looking for all of them just notice which ones occur. For instance I often see when giving a suggestion to a subject in a very deep trance that their eyeball seem to sink into their heads slightly as they take on board the suggestion. Others may twitch slightly a hand, a leg watch carefully for signs and your skills will improve tenfold.

Also look out for frowning, this can often be a sign that the subject did not like the suggestion or did not understand it. In these cases try rephrasing the suggestion and even asking them to nod their head when they understand. Another thing to understand about frowning is it may be part of an abreaction.

In fact any noticeable change to the normal waking state is an indication that the hypnotists suggestions are having some effect. You should be led by these changes and use them to increase or deepen the trance. For example if you notice that the subject's swallowing has increased you should mention it.

When you mention this to him you create for him a self fulfilling prophecy seemingly led by you. I call this LLL **L**ead and be **L**ed into **L**eading. You guide him he responds you read his responses and use them to guide him and so on. This is called a feedback loop. The head nodding mentioned above is also a feedback loop, in fact a very powerful one and should be used regularly.

So you notice your subjects eyes flutter you might say something like 'and as you notice your eyelids begin to flutter you notice you become more deeply relaxed etc'. Because in trance there is no time awareness it seems to the subject that you are telling them to allow their eyelids to flutter and that they will become more deeply relaxed.

Just a few to look out for:

> Eyelids fluttering
>
> Blushing of the skin
>
> Facial muscles completely relaxed
>
> Body completely relaxed
>
> Involuntary twitching
>
> Head dropped forward or to the side

There are dozens and dozens depending on the person. What you are actually looking for is any change at all.

Conditions needed

The conditions needed to enable a subject to enter the hypnotic state again vary depending on the type of hypnosis being implemented and of course the subject himself. We are, though, going to look at the fundamentals first.

First and foremost the hypnotist.

You **MUST** have complete confidence. I cannot stress this enough you must exude confidence in your abilities, you must transfer this confidence to the subject. You must also have the subject confident in the outcome. I.E. they will be hypnotised and the experience will be positive for them, we call this expectancy and belief. If you lack confidence in your abilities the subject will literally feel this through the non verbal signals you send and you will not succeed.

This is why we never TRY hypnosis to SEE it will WORK. Trying something means we are bound to fail. This you will understand later when we discuss Coue's Law of reverse effect and hypnosis depth tests. There is an exception to this try it and see rule, that would be when you are first starting out you may want to practise your newly found skill on a spouse or family member, here you are really trying out the technical parts of your routine rather than trying to see if hypnosis works.

You must also be a leader. You are the master of your craft and you will guide them through the process of being hypnotised. You must create belief and expectancy. The belief and expectation by the subject that something, even if that something is unknown, is going to happen.

So you need your subject to know without doubt that:

You are confident.

You are a leader.

You believe

They believe

They expect

Whilst on the subject of the hypnotist let's look at the most common question, can anyone be a hypnotist? The short answer is yes as already mentioned I have come across plenty of hypnotherapists and stage hypnotists who have obviously done the bare minimum perhaps completed a distance learning course and read a few books and are out there selling their wares.

The more poignant question should be, can anyone be a good hypnotist? The answer to this question is yes if you are willing to work at it!

The truth is some will have to work harder at it than others.

Conditions needed (Rapport)

So after establishing ourselves through our confidence we must build 'Rapport'. This is best described as a state of trust between the hypnotist and the subject. After all you are about to tamper, for want of a better word, with a person's most precious possession, their mind. If trust does not exist between you then you are bound to fail.

It is the job of the hypnotist to build trust and to create rapport between himself and the subject. We do this in many ways. Firstly we must put them at ease generally, confidence again. We must also dispel any misconceptions they may have about hypnosis. Most people's experience will be either from watching Television or having witnessed a stage hypnotist. Explain what hypnosis is and what it is not.

Also to create rapport our body language should be congruent to what we are saying. We can mirror match and pace a subject. To understand this better you will need a very good understanding of non verbal communication which is such huge subject that it cannot be covered completely here.

This is an overview of what is required. As I have already mentioned different emphasis and prerequisites are needed for different types of hypnotism. Below we are going to look at the specific conditions required in each field of hypnosis.

Conditions needed (Therapy)

First and foremost we need a very comprehensive pre-talk.

Understanding exactly what the issue is, also understand how the subject perceives the issue. Take a history and make notes listen to everything being said. Ask questions. Find out how long it has been an issue, and exactly what effect it has on their lives. If you are to be a good therapist you will be using all this information to bring about the desired changes.

Listen to the language they use. You should be using the same language back at them during the trance. If they say that one of the things they hate about smoking is the 'cost implications' be sure to use that same word in context during the session. If you were to change it to say 'financial loss' it would not have the same impact on him as the words 'cost implications'.

Always build rapport, find out what the subject thinks he/she knows about hypnosis. Dispel any fears that they will lose control and that the hypnotist will have absolute power over them. Explain what to expect in trance, that everyone experiences hypnosis in their own way and can often feel as though they were never even hypnotised.

Use the hypnotic 'tests' or 'exercises', explained later, to build a high degree of expectancy and belief. You must take on the role of a leader. You are going to lead them into hypnosis and 'it will happen', remember unshakeable confidence is the first building block to success.

They must have trust, trust in you, trust in your abilities, and trust in a positive outcome. Remember they have come to you with an issue they have, their overall aim is to have a life changing experience. Your aim is to get them there.

The physical setting is important too. The room in which you are to practise the therapy should be comfortable in all aspects. The subject should be comfortable. This is to say that the room should not be too hot or cold. The lighting should be slightly subdued. You should provide a comfortable chair or couch. Ideally there should be no external distractions, however sometimes this is unavoidable. If this is the case use them as part of your induction by simply saying something like. 'Allow the noises of the traffic outside to flow through you helping you to relax even more'. So the mantra here is comfort. Some therapists like to play soft background music. Remember pre conception, expectation and belief.

I mention all these things together because I believe that they are related. Most therapists will tell you that there is a linear structure to a therapy session. I agree that the session should be structured although I disagree that it should be thought of as stages.

Conventional wisdom lists a session as follows:

1. Pre talk

2. Gain Rapport

3. Perform Suggestibility tests

4. Perform induction

5. Perform deepeners

6. Perform depth tests

7. Read script

8. Trance termination

Of course this is the basic format. I on the other hand believe that they should be taken as one task. I think that expectation and belief. By coming to you the subject has done 70% to 90% of your work for you.

All you have to do is keep on increasing the expectation and belief. This is done by convincing them at every stage that what you say will happen will indeed happen. So what we actually have right from the first handshake is a set of convincers. Whether it's doing suggestion tests or pre talk all the time the subject is becoming more convinced. Even on emerging them from the trance the de-brief itself is a convincer.

The more convinced he is the more powerful the effect of the next step and so on. Also remember the deeper they go....the deeper they go. The more suggestible they are the more suggestible they become. Which means that by the time you reach the actual therapy they are so convinced that it has the desired effect.

Conditions needed (Stage)

Again a pre-talk is essential although in the case of stage it needs to be brief and impactful. You have to engage everyone. Those who will be willing subjects and those who remain in the audience are expecting to be entertained

Obviously you are not taking a subjects history so it's all down to you. Explain the do's and don'ts for the audience. Explain what you will and will not be doing without giving too much away. Make sure you cover all your legal bases. Know these off by heart! Most importantly who you will not hypnotise this is usually done in a comedic way.

Explain what is required of them, the volunteers, Concentration etc.

As you'd expect the conditions required for stage hypnosis are very different to that needed for therapy. We still need to build rapport, this we usually do with some form of comedy routine, putting the audience as well as any prospective volunteer at ease. Again we must build belief and expectancy. We should create also an air of awe and nervousness. This may sound counter-productive but believe me it serves a purpose.

On stage we rely heavily on Authority as well as the usual leadership, expectancy and belief etc.

We do not have a subject, instead we should have a volunteer or to be more precise volunteers. Once again the first and most important ingredient is confidence in your ability. We also will be using shock value and rapid inductions

We need highly motivated people, the volunteers should be nervously exited, almost it is said by some, fearful. The audience have come to be entertained or be part of the show

The hypnotist is a showman the whole experience is loud and colourful. Well for the audience anyway!

The physical setup is important too. No loose wires, plenty of space between the play area and the edge of the stage. Enough chairs for everyone. Lighting and sound is very important, after all it's a show. Don't scrimp in this department.

Conditions needed (Street)

Virtually the same as stage except you have fewer, if any, props. Shock, fear and awe best describes what is going on during street hypnosis. Making the volunteers believe in magic and the impossible.

I've toyed with street hypnosis in pubs etc. The big advantage is the intrigue created when you tell people what you do. Once in conversation it is easy to identify potential subjects. They are not the nervous person with issues in your office environment. Also you may not always have a group of people as on stage with varying degrees of suggestibility.

Street hypnosis is probably the easiest and most fun type of all. If you use the rapport techniques described later you can't lose. Incidentally although I say street I really refer to all impromptu hypnosis, such as parties and other social events as well as at a bar.

Conditions needed (Covert)

As mentioned before covert hypnosis is used to get 'victims', and I use this word advisedly, to do with what you will. Not quite against their will but certainly without their permission. What we need for covert hypnosis is a mastery of NLP, distraction and rapport. The whole purpose of this type of hypnosis is that the victim is completely unaware that it ever happened.

Who can be hypnotised

Almost anyone can be hypnotised it is really more a question of how deeply they can be hypnotised and how long it takes to get them under. I believe that everyone that can be hypnotised can be coached into Hyper-Trance. It is merely a question of how long it takes.

In the therapy room the aim is depth, some subjects will be able to achieve a good depth of trance in a reasonable amount of time whilst others may take substantially longer. You must also consider the kind of hypnosis that will bring the best results.

On stage the aim is quite different we are restricted to having a very short period of time and so we are aiming to get the more susceptible of the volunteers to work with.

As mentioned before everyone is different and needs to be treated as individuals, it is worth noting that from a broad perspective there is considered to be two basic types.' Analytical and non-analytical types'.

It is exactly as it sounds the analytical type will question what is going on and likes to keep busy mentally. Instructions given are not necessarily accepted without first analysing them. In the therapy setting we would use distraction and permissive approach to hypnotising them allowing them to keep full control of the situation. On stage they would simply be dismissed as unsuitable. In fact I have found on many occasions that analytical types only volunteer in an attempt to sabotage the show or at least steal the limelight. Get rid of them as soon as you identify them, politely of course!

The non analytical type can easily relax and so just about any approach can be used depending on other characteristics. They are usually much more open to the authoritative methods because they can accept instruction. They make excellent subjects in all circumstances.

Everyone is different. Apart from those who are clinically insane or drunk, everybody is hypnotisable. It is true that the very old and the very young can be more challenging but with perseverance you will get there in the end, as long as they can understand the instructions.

Who can hypnotise (general)

The simple fact is anyone can hypnotise, therefore anyone can be a hypnotist, the more you practice and study the better you'll be. As with all skills practice makes perfect. Some people, it must be said, are seemingly, more gifted than others it is fair to say while there are others who have to work at putting people in trance. This has been compared to the very early beliefs about hypnotism that the hypnotist possesses an animal magnetism which mesmerises the subjects. Complete waffle or fact, no one really knows! Also a good understanding of body language, human behaviour and other peripheral subjects like cold reading and basic magic tricks can be very useful. The more knowledgeable the better.

Who can hypnotise-hypnotic (eyes)

A question I am often asked is whether hypnotists have special hypnotic eyes, and then before I have a chance to answer they usually say something like 'because I have noticed there is something about your eyes that I can't put my finger on'. As I've mentioned previously everything is a convincer and statements like the one above should not be discouraged. When someone makes a statement about you having hypnotic eyes they are starting the process of self convincing.

The actual answer is no you do not need special eyes to be able to hypnotise anyone, it does help if you have a good hypnotic gaze though.

Creating your own compelling hypnotic gaze is quite simple. Stand in front of a mirror about 12 inches (or 30cm for you youngsters) look into the mirror at your own nose then just soften your eyes. By this I mean allow the muscles at the outside of your eyes to relax slightly. Next practice this mirror staring as often as possible until you can do it for long periods without blinking. And that is the hypnotic gaze. This gaze makes people uncomfortable because it seems unnatural and can be a further convincer of your hypnotic abilities.

Who can hypnotise-hypnotic (voice)

Again some people are gifted in this department and some will have to practice. The hypnotic voice you need to use should be different depending on the situation as always. If you look at the teachings of the 'old guard' you will very quickly notice that they refer to a low deep monotone being absolutely necessary to induce a trance state. If you are using progressive relaxation techniques in a therapy room this can, and usually does work, but in my opinion you'd be using a sort of boredom trance induction. The proof of this is the fact that it can take so long.

In today's world of hypnosis it is accepted that your voice should reflect the mood of the situation and must carry the correct weight. It should always be powerful and should resonate from you through the subject. Your voice should carry the emotion of the suggestion right into the subjects being. There must be congruence between what you say and what they feel.

In therapy situation when suggesting relaxation and the like then a low voice is necessary, however it should be used in sort of waves changing to suit the suggestion. For example each time you use a word like deeper or relax you could make your voice slightly deeper and stretch the words out. Conversely if you are saying something like letting go you could also elongate the word but enunciate it in a sort of whimsical way after all you are telling them to let go of something, usually tension.

When it comes to stage or street situations we mostly want to be using authoritative and flamboyant voice patterns. Remember confusion and shock is what we are trying to create and our voice needs to carry this message. Once the usual belief and expectancy is created along with some awe and nervous anticipation the stage hypnotist commands sleep.

Pauses are equally important. They allow time for the suggestion to penetrate and have effect, think of pauses as sinking in time. Without pauses the subconscious may not have time enough to assimilate new information.

Who can hypnotise (Personal)

It is also worth mentioning general presentation. If you intend to be a therapist being overweight and or a smoker are not conducive, after all imagine going to a therapist for help with stopping smoking or weight control and meeting a therapist who was obese and or smoking. You should always be smart and well groomed remember everything is a convincer and first impressions should be the first step in that direction.

The same applies to the stage and street hypnotist you should be of smart appearance well groomed with impeccable personal hygiene. Also you must have the right persona. That is to say a supremely confident showman. After all in street and stage it's a show from the moment you start until you have completely finished.

Be prepared and practice

In conclusion to this chapter I would like to mention a few of the most important skills you should possess. Putting people into trance either with their prior knowledge or not is very easy. In fact some would say too easy, what you must know is how to correctly end a trance and bring the subject back to the here and now (emergence, termination or awakening) also how to deal with any abreaction if one were ever to occur. Even if you only ever become an average hypnotist you absolutely must be an expert at these two things.

Abreaction.

The expression and consequent release of a previously repressed emotion, achieved through reliving the experience that caused it.

It happens when the subject is regressed back to a time in their lives when there was a dramatic incident of some description. The memory can be so vivid that they feel they are actually there.

To deal with an abreaction simply say the following.

'Leave that memory behind as you come back to the here and now'.

To safeguard against abreactions use the expression 'as if', so you would say something like 'it is as if you were six years old' instead of 'imagine you are six years old'. It is a subtle but important difference.

Another safety measure is to make a safe place. It can be the chair they are sitting in. Then as well as leaving the memory we can return them to a safe place, also tell them early on that they will always be able to hear your voice and understand what you are saying.

Do not touch the subject if they experience an abreaction!

Signs of abreaction can range from very subtle to quite dramatic. The subject may just look a bit uncomfortable or be sobbing uncontrollably.

One last word

Practice, Practice, Practice.

CHAPTER ~ 2 ~ PRE-TALK

What is a pre-talk

Well the fact that someone has either come to you for therapy or volunteered to be on stage is the first convincer then the pre-talk is the second convincer. Except in the case of street where your first opportunity at a convincer is your introduction and as for covert, well it wouldn't be very covert if you announced to the victim you are a hypnotist.

The pre-talk is exactly what it says. It's what you do pre hypnosis. You should use it to gauge any person who you think you should not hypnotise. Dispel any misconceptions, build rapport and convince the subject of your abilities. Give them all the information they need to be successfully hypnotised.

It is also used for you to make your mind up about the best approaches for you to use, which type of induction etc.

pre-talks should always lead seamlessly into the susceptibility tests!

Different pre-talk prerequisites

Laid out below are the differing pre-talk conditions you should be aiming at.

Pre-talk Therapy

Inform the client that there is nothing mysterious about hypnosis. Give them a short history lesson regarding ancient cultures and meditation around the world. Tell them about what to expect during the session. Ask them questions about what they think hypnosis is and educate them. Tell them about depths of hypnosis. Have them fill out a history of their condition.

Pre-talk Stage

Again the pre-talk should be information based. No history lesson here though. We need to make it fairly brief and to the point remember you are there to entertain. They have after all come for the show and some to be part of it. Create lots of expectation and belief and let them know what is required of them. Also you will need some sort of verbal disclaimer. Volunteers need to be making an informed choice before they effectively make fools of themselves in front of friends, family and the public. Above all start convincing.

Pre-talk Street

Virtually the same as stage but since they have not come to you it's all about the pre-talk being from scratch as a persuader to get volunteers.

Pre-talk Covert

Pre-talk what pre-talk. There is no pre-talk with covert hypnosis since the victim is or at least should be completely unaware that they are being put into a suggestive state.

Sample pre-talks

Now the interesting stuff starts. These are a sample of what you should actually say and are in italics. Don't worry, the entire uninterrupted sequences are to be found at the end of the book so you can just print them off or photocopy them. As you will notice the therapy pre-talk is quite long and should be. As well as the words you will be using matching mirroring leading techniques to help create and maintain rapport. The stage should be a lot shorter you can only hold an audience's attention for so long. The street is even shorter the idea is to get subjects ensnared before they've really had time to think about it.

Sample pre-talk Therapy

"Hypnosis is a kind of altered state of consciousness, your subconscious becomes very open to suggestion, when you are in this state you can make positive changes to just about anything in your life. Most people who have experienced it say that it is like daydreaming and that it is very pleasant. You are aware of everything that goes on at no time are you out of control. I am only here as a sort of guide to help you to hypnotise yourself because all hypnosis is really self hypnosis.

In fact just about everyone is hypnotisable some people go very deep and others not, so some take quite a bit of time and others achieve it very quickly. As I have mentioned it is just a sort of daydream state and we all daydream, sometimes we daydream several times a day. In hypnosis we just sort of extend the time of the daydream to suit us

You cannot be made to do things that you don't want to do. You may have seen a stage show on TV or even live and thought that the people on stage lose control that the hypnotist has some power over them. Those people have volunteered themselves and are game for a laugh but could stop anytime they really wanted. You retain your basic morals and beliefs and if I made a suggestion that was in conflict with those you would simply wake up. So you can't be made to hurt yourself or anyone.

You cannot be made to divulge any secrets, in fact it is why hypnotism is not used as a reliable source for a confession in court.

Another thing that some people may think is that you can get stuck in trance. Well you cannot get stuck in hypnotic trance you do not go into a deep sleep like the princess in the fairy tale. In fact if I use the word sleep it just refers to that daydream state where your eyes are closed and your body and mind are completely relaxed.

Are there any other things you'd like to know about hypnosis?

Describe to me what it is that you have come here for today."

You of course already know what the main issue is but it is useful to have them give you as much detail possible. This will help you to formulate or tailor the session to their particular needs. Use the same words as them for instance if a smoker says words like costly, disgusting and harmful be sure to use the exact same words when carrying out the therapy later. A written history is best.

"Good and so we can help with that. It should take no longer than...sessions."

Remember to be confident and empathetic as if helping them to achieve their goal is an absolute forgone conclusion (belief and expectancy)

"Do you have any further questions? Good and are you ok to do the hypnosis now. Good let's begin. I don't know if it will happen straight away or it will take a minute."

This again is a great convincer, a double bind presupposing hypnosis in no more than a minute or two.

Go straight to convincer number three the suggestibility tests

Sample pre-talk Stage

This is a show and this thought should be foremost in your mind at all times. Keep it light hearted. Now is the time to heighten the belief and expectancy and some excitement. The awe and nervousness will come in the suggestibility tests.

"Good evening everyone my name is Steve Leap...tonight be prepared to be amazed not by me because I am not the star of the show. No tonight ladies and gentlemen you are the stars of the show!"

Sweep your hand across the audience.

"Soon I will be asking for volunteers to join me on stage. Even those of you who do not volunteer beware because now that you have heard my voice and seen my eyes you may go into trance at anytime!"

If done with enough showmanship and confidence you will have already started to create the awe and nervous tension you so badly need.

"To be hypnotised is very simple in fact many experts believe that all hypnosis is merely self hypnosis. To be hypnotised you need to be capable of four things. ICIF a good IMAGINATION...Good powers of CONCENTRATION...Be reasonably INTELLIGENT...and be able to FOLLOW instructions.

There are a few people I am not allowed to hypnotise those are people who are drunk."

This usually gets a big cheer.

"Anyone with mental health issues or serious health issues of any kind."

Quite often a good laugh again.

"Pregnant women, anyone high on drugs or anyone under the age of eighteen.

If you fit into any of the above categories please do not volunteer!

Hypnosis is a quite natural state whereby a person in trance is highly suggestible and that just about anything is possible."

Depending on the audience and or the type of show you have billed you may want to add.

"No one will be taking their clothes this is a family show. "

You now can either ask for volunteers or start the suggestibility tests with the entire audience.

Sample pre-talk Street

If doing street hypnosis from cold say at a private party where no one knows what I do I usually set the scene rather than introduce myself as a hypnotist. It's much more fun and in my experience more successful all round. Remember you've got to create rapport, belief, expectancy and interest all in your (seemingly) impromptu pre talk. Ideally do this with a group.

What is it you do to make a crust. Ask all of them, show interest in all their answers and make even the most mundane job sound important. That is make the person feel important (emotion over logic) Mirror and match each person as they speak in order to build rapport. Try to hold the fact that you are a hypnotist to your chest as long as possible. When you finally make your announcement, be prepared, people are usually very interested and you could very quickly become the centre of attention. You will be asked all sorts of questions. This is the time to do the pre-talk. Assuming you've had all the usual questions it would go something like this:

"Well it's nothing more than a sort of guided meditation really. Everybody does it all the time like daydreaming. Have you ever driven your car somewhere on say a regular journey and when you arrive you think to yourself how the heck did I get here?"

You will almost certainly get a lot of nods in agreement.

"Well that's a very light form of hypnosis. Your subconscious mind has driven you home and your conscious mind has been doing the important things in the here and now, like wondering what's for dinner or what's on the TV later. The only difference is that when you get hypnotised by a professional like myself is that you get expert guidance to make the very most of the experience. In fact

people have told me the feeling they get when hypnotised is so good it's like the second best feeling they've ever had."

Usually someone or more likely several people will ask how it works. When this happens you've got your volunteers. At this point I don't generally say hey you want to try it. This has a tendency to scare people off. Instead I continue along these lines.

"Well I can show you a couple of tricks if you like."

This brings a few ok's on nearly every occasion and so you start with some suggestibility tests. As I start the tests I just do one last thing and that's the disclaimers, the final part of the pre-talk

"Just want to make sure you're not pregnant, or on any kind of drugs, legal or otherwise, and that you are over eighteen, that you are of sound mind and body?"

CHAPTER ~ 3 ~ SUSCEPTIBILITY EXERCISES

Purpose

The purpose of susceptibility, or as sometimes known, suggestibility tests is to ascertain how easily and/or deeply a subject is likely to be hypnotised once the process starts. When used properly they not only provide the hypnotist with valuable information but can also act as yet another powerful convincer. Regardless of how a subject 'performs' these tests never allow them to think they have failed.

As mentioned before once you start with the pre-talk everything is part of the induction. Therefore the so called 'tests' are just the next step in the process. Remember the more the subject follows the suggestion the more suggestible they become, the more suggestible they become the more convinced and so on. If you use what are known as guaranteed tests then you are actually convincing them that not only will they be good subjects but also that they are already beginning to be hypnotised. Therefore depending on how much time you have and the general circumstances you should be using as many tests/ convincers as you can.

Never tell a subject that they have failed a test. In fact it is probably better never to mention the word test at all. If you use the word test then there is potential for failure. If they do not respond well to one of your suggestions during this step not only will they not be convinced but also all the belief and expectancy you have carefully instilled will be gone. The law of reversed effect coming into play only this time to your disadvantage.

The usual tests include magnetic fingers, hand lock, eye lock and body sway. This is by no means a comprehensive list. These are just the most common ones. Just as with inductions and deepening's you can be as inventive as you like with suggestibility tests. The point is as always to gauge how well the subject responds and how quickly as well as convincing them that 'something' is happening.

Another important factor is that it is usually better to use a permissive tone and language when conducting these tests in a therapy situation. You should always nurture the idea that they are in control. Remember they have come to you for help and guidance. In a stage environment authority is needed. Here we rely much more on shock and awe as well as belief and expectancy to convince the subjects and of course you are dealing with a group as well as a possibly rowdy group of spectators.

Therapy

In a therapy setting when using tests it is always advisable to tell the subject that you are using these techniques to train them in the art of hypnosis. Remember never say test, if you tell them that it is simply part of the process of them learning to let go and that you are instructing them in how best to use their own imagination and concentration, you will find that the job of hypnotising them becomes infinitely more easy. If you reinforce each test with praise etc it only convinces them further.

Stage

With stage shows we must remember, I know I keep reminding you, we are there to entertain. Doing endless tests in order to make sure everyone is on the same page as it were, is simply not practicable. Time is of the essence. Therefore we need to do the tests as quickly as possible in order to find our most likely candidates. Once you have your volunteers on stage you need to find the best subjects and keep them for the inductions and deepeners.

At this point it is best to do what I call a crossover from the pre-talk. Tell them that although just about everyone is hypnotisable different styles suit different people and that also some people take longer than others. It is a lot easier then to use the word test and to dismiss, gracefully the less susceptible volunteers. You can explain this during the pre-talk but you will most likely find you have a lot less volunteers in the first place. Those that do volunteer will be more likely to want to comply with the tests yet again because you have challenged them convincing themselves

Street

With regard to street hypnosis there is no real difference between test/ inductions/ deepeners etc. In reality once you've completed a pre-talk it's all hypnosis. One thing blurs into the next and so on. In fact if you wanted proof that everything is a convincer see for yourself after completing this book, you will see exactly what I mean for yourself.

Sample Tests

In this section I am not going to distinguish between which tests should be used under different circumstances because they are all relevant. In fact it's about which suit your style more.

NOTE:

From here on when you see the dotted lines after or before words or groups of words they indicate a pause the more dots.... the longer the pause!

Magnetic fingers

This can be done sitting or standing

"Hold your hands out in front of you clasp your hands together and interlock your fingers except your index fingers. Point your index fingers out straight away from you and keep them about an inch apart."

Help them do this it gets the right position quickly and creates compliance. Also start to employ your hypnotic vocal tones.

"Focus all your concentration directly at the space in between your fingers....

And notice how the two fingers are being attracted towards each other...

Allow yourself to imagine that your fingers are like powerful magnets

Being attracted to each other...

Don't force it just let it happen...

I don't know if it will happen immediately or if it will take a little time...

Whatever is right for you...

And as I talk to you and you concentrate you find that...

Those fingers are getting closer and closer and closer together...

The gap between those fingers getting smaller and smaller...

There notice how much closer they are getting....

It's just as if those fingers are being magnetically pulled towards each other.

Closer.....closer.....and closer.

Comfortably moving closer together all the time..."

Keep repeating variations of the above until the fingers touch remember the feedback loop. Once you see movement encourage it

"You see...

Now they are touching.

Did you think that would work for you?

That's the power of your mind. How amazing is that?"

This is an ideal first test and convincer and is guaranteed to work for anyone who is not deliberately resisting. The reason it works every time is because with the hands and fingers in this position it is impossible to keep the fingers apart. The subject does not know this of course and is usually quite surprised believing that something hypnotic, or at least strange has just happened. Because of this it is a powerful first convincer and sets the subject up for more success in any following tests.

I recommend using this as the first test in almost all circumstances. As well as Identifying receptive subjects and helping to convince it has an added bonus of weeding out potentially resistant subjects. In the stage environment make a note of anyone whose fingers did not move and if they remain resistant in subsequent tests you can dismiss them and concentrate on the more susceptible.

In the therapy room any resistance to tests may be indications that the person is not following instructions correctly. Maybe there is something lacking in other areas of your pre-talk or your own confidence. You may not have spent enough time creating expectancy and belief.

If this happens do not tell the person they have failed this will only compound the problem. Explain to them that they have just proved to themselves that they have the willpower to stay in control and that this is a good thing. However the purpose of them being there is to achieve and to do that they need to use their Intelligence, Concentration and Imagination. To be able to do this and to attain their goals they must listen carefully and follow your instructions.

Hand Clasp Test

This is preferably done with their hands up in front of their faces with their palms and arms touching although they can have their hands out in front of them at waist height.

"Everyone look at me. I want you to put your hands out in front of you and lock your elbows. Now place your palms together and interlock your fingers like so."

Demonstrate by doing it yourself and reinforce the compliance by physically moving their hands slightly

"Now look at your hands and use all of your imagination and concentration....

Squeeze the palms of your hands together as hard as you can

And press your fingers into the backs of your hands as hard as you can too....

Now whilst you are pressing firmly I want you to imagine...

That there is the worlds strongest superglue between your palms bonding your hands together....

At the same time that same superglue is on your fingers...

And is starting to stick your fingers to the back of your hands...

As I speak I want you to now start to imagine your fingers and your hands are becoming stuck together....

Becoming so tightly stuck together it's as if your hands and fingers are made from one piece of material....

As if they were like one piece of solid wood....

That they have become glued together...

As you imagine that piece of solid wood...

I want you feel your hands becoming more and more stuck together....

In fact they are so tightly stuck together...

That if you were to try to pull them apart you would find it impossible....

In fact they have become so tightly stuck together...

So solid that when you try to pull them apart...

They simply stick even tighter....

When I count from one to three they will be so tightly stuck together...

That the harder you try to separate them the harder it becomes the more stuck they are....

ONE...sticking tighter and tighter!

TWO...hands stuck tightly together!

THREE...completely stuck!

The harder you try to pull them apart the more stuck they become....

You cannot pull them apart!

Try but you cannot pull them apart you cannot pull them apart!!

Stop trying now....

Now your arms your fingers and hands become unglued....

Pull them apart as they are now quite normal again...."

Note that you must return them to normality. In fact from their point of view their hands stuck because you <u>told</u> them and they released because of your <u>permission</u>. Convincer anyone? To add to this compliance and convincer you can gently push their hands apart with your finger between their wrist as you give the instruction

This can be done with the eyes open or closed. When doing a stage authoritarian style I prefer eyes open since it has more impact on the subject, they are more in awe of what's happening. It is always better under these conditions to have the hands up in front of the face. This is for two reasons. One it is harder to separate the hands if the elbows are touching, Two with their hands right in front of their face their eyes are focused intently on their hands and not the audience.

Eye lock/ catalepsy

Do this one sitting down or standing.

"Make yourself as comfortable as you can...

Take a really deep breath...."

Take a breath with them. Leading and pacing them. Do this with all their breaths

"Take another really deep breath and hold it for five seconds....

Now take one last deep breath and hold it again for five seconds

Good and as you breathe out just allow your eyes to close....

And relax...

And as you allow your eyes to relax I want you to concentrate on your eyes...

Allow your full attention to focus on your eyes and in particular your eyelids.....

And the muscles that control your eyelids....

Yes all those tiny muscles all around your eyes and eyelids....

Those tiny muscles that when they tense and tighten cause your eyelids to open....

Think of those muscles and think of relaxing those muscles....

Relax those muscles so much that they won't open...

Keep concentrating on all those tiny muscles and how comfortably relaxed you can make them..."

.....Pause for five seconds.....

Good now I want you to Imagine what it will be like if your eyelids...

Were so relaxed that they won't open...

Really focus on imagining what that sensation would be like...

That sensation of your eyelids being so completely comfortably relaxed that they just won't work...

And when you know that you have relaxed the muscles around your eyes and eyelids...

When you are certain that they are so relaxed that they will not open you can go ahead and try...

When you know they are so relaxed they will not work...

Not until you are absolutely sure that they won't work...

And once you are sure that they won't work you can try to open them...

That's right you can try to open them but the harder you try the more they just stay closed...

The harder you try the harder it is to open them...

The harder you try the more relaxed they become...

That's it when you're ready try...

Try to open your eyes it is impossible...

Stop trying...

And now as I count to three your eyes and eyelids return to normal.

One ...two...three...."

This is a wonderful test since it combines the double bind and the law of reversed effect. Because you tell them only to try to open their eyes when they know for sure they won't open and also the harder they try the harder it will be. This is a brilliant double power convincer.

It should be noted that this is a variation on the theme of the first part of the Elman induction technique and you could easily use this test to lead straight into a powerful induction. Actually this is true of all so called tests.

Light heavy arms

I find this test is best done seated.

"Put your arms out straight in front of you...

Have the palm of your right hand facing down toward the ground.

With the palm of your left hand facing upwards toward the ceiling, like this."

Demonstrate the position.

"In a moment...not yet...when I tell you I want you to take three deep breaths.

And as you exhale on the third breath I'm going to get you to close your eyes..."

One thing to note about tests is that even though you can perform them with the subject having their eyes open each time they successfully complete a test they are already entering trance. Just not the classic eyes closed slumped position.

"Imagine that tied to your left hand is a Piece of string...

On the other end of the piece of string is a large red balloon...

Full of helium...

At the same time Imagine that in your left hand is a stack of library books...

Very heavy old library books...

And as those heavy library books begin to weigh down on your left hand...

So the red balloon starts to pull your right hand up...

Feel it rising slowly into the air...

Good as you can feel me place more books in your left hand...

And your left hand begins to go down and down...

Your right hand and arm rising all the time...

Because your left hand and arm are moving down...

More and more...

Left hand down...

Right arm up...

Now open your eyes."

Keep repeating the instructions until there is movement. At this point the two arms should have moved in the directions you have suggested. The better the subject the greater the distance will be between the hands.

Body Sway

Get them to stand feet together hands at their sides. Stand behind them with the outside of your foot up against their heels. Put your hands on their shoulders and tell them to keep their body as rigid as possible.

Now move them around gently by the shoulders making sure they are following your instructions.

Then let go of their shoulders and continue with the verbal suggestions.

"Take a deep breath and hold it for a second...

Good let it go...

Take another deep breath and hold it again...

And let go...

And one more time a really deep breath...

Hold...

And let it go...

Good as I stand behind you I want you to imagine...

That there is a magnetic force building up...

A force that is pulling you backwards...

Feel it pulling you further and further...

Just allow it to happen...

Don't worry I won't let you fall...

Just allow yourself...

Feel yourself being pulled back more and more..."

Repeat these instructions over and over compounding the effect by changing the wording slightly until eventually they fall back. Be sure to catch them.
The body sway test above is written in standalone format.
However if you were performing this test after completing other successful tests you can shorten it down to the following.

"Stand up straight take a deep breath. I am going to stand behind you. I want you to just let whatever happens happen. I'm not sure what will happen but when it does don't worry I won't let you fall. I'll be back here to catch you. OK?"

You leave them and in a short while usually under 15 seconds they will fall back into your arms. This can also lead to a shock or instant induction.

CHAPTER ~ 4 ~ INDUCTIONS

What is an induction?

This is where we get to the meat of the subject. An in induction is exactly what it says. It is the process of helping, guiding or inducing the subject into the state of hypnosis. The aim of an induction is to induce the light hypnotic state. There are as many ways to achieve this as there are stars in the night sky. As you can probably imagine different situations call for different styles of induction. The rule of thumb is the quicker someone enters trance the deeper they go the trade off is that they can come out quite easily if deepenrs are not used quickly afterwards.

Although the actual induction, and by that, I mean the words and or props used, are a matter of preference for the individual hypnotist. The 'style' of the induction is determined by the expectations of the subject or audience. This may sound a bit upside down but when you think it through it makes perfect sense. The situation you are in, the pre-talk you have given will give the subjects an overall picture of what to expect and believe. If you add to this their preconceptions garnered from TV and films etc you can start to see what I mean.

For example it would be wholly inappropriate to drop someone backwards on to the floor, as you have probably seen on TV or at a stage show, in a consulting room when your intention is to carry out some form of therapy. In the same breath you would definitely not want to take half hour or more inducing trance in a stage setting since by the time you get the subjects deeply entranced enough to do your comedy routines the night would be over not to mention most of the audience would probably have left or gone to sleep through sheer boredom.

If someone expects you to use a pocket watch then do it. Feeding into their expectation helps the process.

So armed with this information let's look at the different types of induction and when they are most commonly used.

Induction types for various situations

Therapy

Most commonly used would be some kind of progressive relaxation technique or PRI for short. This is the traditional 'you are feeling sleepy' type of induction we all remember from cartoons etc from our childhood. There are of course variations on this theme with the classic boredom right through to the currently popular visualisation techniques. They all achieve the light stage of hypnosis by putting the 'critical factor' to sleep or if not to sleep at least into a state where it doesn't really care what's going on.

Stage

For stage, instant and rapid inductions are the way to go. As the names suggest these inductions take very little or even no time at all. We use shock, awe and fear to achieve these kinds of inductions. Sometimes in stage inductions we use an amount of PRI as a bridge from the suggestibility tests to the instant or rapid induction, especially when dealing with large groups. We achieve the 'light hypnotic state' by means of shock. As each person on stage goes into trance so the next in line becomes more susceptible. So even if you start with a short PRI by the time you have hypnotised the first few the rest will go under instantly.

Street

For street any type of induction that takes your liking really. It is literally all down to personal preference. This will depend on the pre-talk and the personality of the subject. In the street setting there is a tendency to use hypnosis as a demonstration of magic. Creating expectancy is the key and so whatever you get the subject to expect will guide the induction sequence. It's quite common to use the suggestibility tests and convincer as the actual induction.

Covert

Rapid induction is the key here. And the style is most definitely confusion and distraction. Here we give the conscious so much to do that we overload the critical factor and it temporarily says to itself 'leave me alone for a while this is too much.

Sample inductions

Now that we understand the types of induction let's look at some samples.

A classic therapy induction.

Focus their attention and bore them to sleep. Well sort of, progressive relaxation induction.

Remember these inductions should be done straight after the suggestibility tests.

"Pick a point on the ceiling and look up at that point. Do not take your eyes off it for a moment. As you sit there looking at the ceiling I want you to become aware of your body. In a moment I'm going to get you to take three deep breaths. Not yet in a moment. I'm going to get you to breathe in as deeply as you can through your nose. Then I want you to hold your breath while I count to three. Then I want you to breathe out through your mouth gently and slowly. Do you understand?"

Wait for confirmation

"OK keeping your eyes firmly fixed on that point on the ceiling...

Take a nice deep breath in...

Now hold it...1...2...3 ...

And exhale...

And again take a nice deep breath in...

Hold it...1...2...3....

And exhale...

And one more time...

Breathe in...

Hold it...1...2..3...

And exhale...

Good...

You probably already noticed that you feel a bit more relaxed...

Generally because whenever we breathe out...

Our body tends to relax a little bit...

It's just that we are not usually aware of it.

In a moment I'm going to ask you to do this breathing exercise three more times...

And this time each time you breathe out...

I want you to notice that feeling of relaxation on each out breath..

Good take a nice deep breath in...

And hold it...1...2...3...

And slowly exhale feeling that wave of relaxation as the air passes across your lips...

Feel your whole body relax...

That's it good.....

And again take a really deep breath all the way down...

Hold it...1...2...3...

And exhale...

And as you exhale feel yourself becoming more relaxed...

And one last time...

Breathe in slowly through your nose deeper and deeper...

And hold...1...2...3...

And breathe out slowly releasing any remaining tension...

Now that you are completely relaxed...

I want you to think about your toes...

And as you think about your toes...

Imagine they are becoming more relaxed as if they were twice as relaxed...

Feel any tension just melt away...

And take that feeling of relaxation and allow it to move up through your feet...

Feel the deep relaxation in every part of your feet top and bottom...

Good...

I want you now to let that feeling spread up through from your toes and feet...

All the way up through your shins and calves right up to your knees...

As you feel that relaxation allow it to spread...

Further up through the tops of your legs all the way to your waist...

So from your toes right up to your waist is completely relaxed...

Now take that relaxation and feel it spread further up through your chest and back...

And along your shoulders and arms too...

Feel that pleasant wonderful feeling of relaxation right from your toes...

Through your entire body up to your neck...

Enjoy this feeling and allow it to move from your neck and around your head...

All the way around the back of your head...

And at the same time up across your face...

And all the way to your eyes....

Feel now all the muscles around your eyes relaxing...

And as they relax...

You feel your eyes becoming...

Heavier...

Heavier and heavier as all the tiny muscles let go of any remaining tension...

And the eye lids just close. "

You now have a hypnotised subject ready for the next stages in the process.

Stage induction.

If you have created the correct atmosphere of expectancy and belief it can be as simple as telling someone to sleep.

Look them straight in the eye and say in a loud commanding voice SLEEP! This of course is an 'instant induction' and all the circumstances will need to be perfect. If you are a beginner it is unlikely you will be using this method.

It is more likely you will be using various 'rapid inductions'. The example below is a very reliable method commonly known as 'handshake induction'. As you can imagine it does what it says on the tin!

If you use the right tests in the right order, as we will discuss in the 'putting it all together section', you can flow effortlessly from them into the induction and it will take very little time.

Have the subject face you either seated or standing. For first time hypnotists I would suggest seated for safety reasons. Offer your hand up as if for a handshake. As the subject puts their hand forward, gently but quickly take their wrist with your left hand and bring their hand up in front of their face about two to three inches away from their nose as you do make the following suggestions.

"Look at your hand...

In particular focus on the differences in the skin tone...

Because as you notice the various subtle variations...

You begin to notice other things...

Like the number of lines in the skin...

And you can focus on one of those lines...

And as you focus on that line...

You begin to notice that your hand is starting to move down...

Away from your face...

And as that happens....

In your own time...

Because as your hand slowly drops...

So your head drops...

And you feel your eyes closing...

As if the eyelids were just too...

Heavy to stay open...

As if they were just too relaxed to bother to stay open...

And as they close you feel yourself relax completely. "

Street

For the street you must keep a sense of fun at all times. To this end here we will look at a comical induction which not only onlookers will find amusing but even the subject will.

Get the subject to stand upright with their feet shoulder width apart with the heel of the left foot in line with the toes of the right. Get them to bend their knees ever so slightly and to look at their left foot. As they look down walk around behind them and stand next to them on their left side. Put your right hand around their back and onto their shoulder and just gently pull them to the left, just so that their centre of gravity is to the left and forward of the centre of their body. This should all be done in a subtle and conversational way. As you perform these physical actions you say to them.

"I want you to look at your left foot...

let me come around to that side..."

This is when you carry out the physical movement from the previous paragraph

"OK focus on that foot ...

Really look at it...

And as you look at it...

I want you to use your imagination...

I know you have a fantastic imagination from the exercises we just did...

So really focus down and imagine that you have just stepped on a tube of the strongest..

Fastest acting glue in the world...

And as you look you can actually feel that glue taking effect...

It's starting to bond the bottom of your shoe...

To the floor...

You can actually feel your foot becoming stuck...

To...

The...

Floor...

Sticking tighter and tighter...

The more you look the more stuck it becomes...

The glue is so strong that if you try to lift your foot...

It won't budge...

In fact the harder you try to lift it...

The harder it is...

The harder you try the more stuck it becomes...

Try and you cannot...

Try and you cannot lift your foot...

Stop trying.

Now take their hand it doesn't matter which. Place it on their head and say.

Just as your foot is stuck to the floor you find that when I let go of your hand...

It too will be stuck...

Look it's stuck...

I can take it off...

But when I place it on your head...

It immediately becomes stuck just as strongly stuck as your foot is to the floor...

Now I am going to count to three...

And as soon as I reach three your hand will become normal again and you can put it down.....one....two...three...

Hand back to normal."

Now stand behind them and put your hands on their shoulders and as you say the words below gently pull them up so that they are completely upright.

"And as I count to three again...

Your foot will return completely back to normal and you will be able to move it...

One...

Two...

Three...

Foot back to normal...

Right sit down and close your eyes...

And as soon as your eyes are closed they will become tightly stuck together...

Just as your foot stuck to the floor...

And your hand stuck to your head...

Your eyes are now closed and will not open...

Try and open them and they will not...

The harder you try the tighter they become...

Stop trying and sleep."

CHAPTER ~ 5 ~ DEEPENING

Why deepen

The purpose of the deepening is, as the name suggests is to deepen the degree of trance beyond the light trance state achieved by the induction. Deepening of the trance occurs in two ways.

One is deliberate and is done immediately after the induction. The second however is the natural deepening that occurs during any hypnotic trance. This occurs as a kind of self serving loop. As a suggestion is received and acted upon this is in effect a convincer and makes the subject more suggestible and therefore more deeply hypnotised. This is especially so if we do as previously mentioned and use the head nod feedback compliance.

It's the reason that stage performers start with simple comedy routines and work their way up to more difficult ones as well as using fewer and fewer subjects along the way.

Also under therapy conditions we can perform deliberate testing again starting with simple suggestions working up to more complicated ones. The depth tests have the added bebifit of being deepeners within themselves.

We are going to look at structured deepeners used immediately after the induction. When I say immediately it is worth repeating, that the entire session or show should actually flow as one. First though it is worth mentioning this:

The deeper you go the better you feel and the better you feel the deeper you go

It's the ultimate self serving internalised feedback loop. Say this during the deepeners and or the sketches or scripts and the subject will gradually move further into trance. Also you can mention that the sound of your voice as well as sounds around them even the clicking of your fingers all serve to take them deeper. In fact any trigger you like.

Sample Deepeners

Therapy

The sample deepener I am going to describe for therapy is very common and very useful since it implies depth by its very nature. It is called the staircase deepener. It is important to keep as many of the senses involved and make the process as rich as possible. You should be like a novelist describing the scene you wish to portray in as much detail as possible and just like the novelist your subject will be lost in the story or as we say focussed.

Remember this is done directly after you have completed the induction

"And your eyelids close...

I want you to imagine you are standing at the top of a staircase on a landing...

You look down and see that the staircase itself is very well lit..

You look to the side a see a very sturdy hand rail...

See yourself reaching out and putting your hand on the rail...

That's right and you feel just how strong the rail is...

In a moment I am going to count from ten down to one...

And as I count down I want you to walk down the steps...

One at a time with each number...

OK nod your head when you understand...

Ten step onto the first step and as you do feel that feeling of moving down...

And nine, going down onto the next step...

And when you step onto that step feel yourself relaxing becoming more comfortable...

Eight going down feeling more relaxed...

Seven...

As if you meant to go twice as deeply relaxed...

Six...

Down onto the next step because five takes you even further into relaxation...

It's as if with each step you become twice as deeply relaxed twice as comfortable...

Be...four...

You go down deeper and deeper and three just makes you feel so relaxed...

Two be more relaxed than you have ever felt...

And down now...

Right down to the bottom and...

One you are at the bottom you can be more relaxed...

More comfortable than you have ever been."

Stage

Since time is of the essence on stage the structured deepener needs to be done in a fairly short time. Remember once the volunteers start following suggestions they will become more suggestible. In the therapy situation we hypnotise and deepen the subjects trance and then we carry out the therapy. On the stage the deepeners are actually part of the show itself.

"That's right you have used your excellent powers of intelligence, concentration and imagination...

To become relaxed...

I want you to concentrate a bit more...

I'm going to count from 10 down to 1 and as I count I want you to Picture each number as I say it...

And when I say gone let the number disappear and as you do relax your body even further..."

NOD YOUR HEAD WHEN YOU UNDERSTAND...

"10...

Picture the number 10...

And gone...

Relax...9...

And gone...8...

Gone and allow yourself to continue relax every single muscle and fibre in your body...

7...and gone...

6...still relaxing as the number has gone...

5...gone...

4...........gone.....

3............ and because it's gone it just serves to take you deeper and deeper...

So deep......2.....

Gone.......and 1........

All numbers gone....

Down to every fibre and tissue of your being...

Every muscle completely relaxed...

And from now on for the rest of this evening....

Every word that I say every sound you hear just serves to take you deeper...

Especially laughter and applause....

Each time you hear laughter or applause it's as if you go twice as deep as before...

Nod your head when you understand..."

Turn to your audience and say.

"Please give everyone on stage a huge round of applause......as they just continue to go deeper and deeper."

Street

The way we deepen in street hypnosis is by just continuing to give convincers. You already had their feet stuck, then their hand. So you just continue each time they comply they become deeper in trance and more suggestible.

"I'm going to lift your arm and hold it out in front of you...
As soon as I let go you will find it is stuck there...
You cannot move it...
The harder you try the more rigid it becomes...
If I tap it...
It will just bounce back...
There you see...
If I take hold of your arm it will move for me...
But as soon as I let go it locks into place exactly where I let go of it..."

You can continue like this for as long as you like or till the joke wears thin. This is in fact the essence of street hypnosis. As you can see whatever you suggest happens. If you chose to move it along further then most commonly you would perform seeming magic tricks.

NOTE:

You will have noticed that the term 'nod your head when you understand' is used quite frequently. This is done because when they do they are agreeing to carry out the suggestion. You are not saying 'if' you understand but 'when' you understand.

CHAPTER ~ 6 ~ DEPTH TESTING

Purpose of testing

Following the induction and the initial deepeners it is essential for the hypnotist to test the depth of hypnosis in the subject. Remember depth of hypnosis relates directly to the suggestibility of the subject. Depth testing is not only an indicator of how deeply hypnotised a subject is, it also has the effect of actually deepening the trance. Each time a test is 'passed' the more suggestible the subject becomes because of the inherent convincer.

Again we would use depth testing in different ways depending on the situation. In the therapy room we use them in a very structured manner in order to ascertain and obtain a suitable level of suggestibility for us to carry out the actual therapy element. If a subject is too lightly hypnotised suggestions may not be acted upon as desired. It is always preferable to have the subject as deeply in trance as possible in order to make changes.

On stage or on the street deepeners are actually a part of the sketches themselves. They serve to move the subject into deeper trance states as well as keeping the audience entertained. The more suggestible they become the more difficult tasks they will be able to perform. We would also use a complete compliance statement on stage

Formal depth testing for different stages of hypnosis follows a simple pattern. We do a simple test. The subject complies with the suggestion this serves to convince them of their trance state. Then in turn it makes them more open to suggestion and so when a more difficult test is suggested and compliance is achieved it helps to convince yet again and so it goes. The tests become increasingly harder and harder.

Formal depth tests

Light Trance

>Eye Catalepsy

>Arm Catalepsy

Medium Trance

>Multiple muscle group catalepsy

>Analgesia

Deep Trance

>Positive hallucination

Hyper Trance

>Negative hallucination

Sample depth tests therapy

"In a moment I'm going to lift up your arm in front of you...
Now imagine that the elbow is locked...
And now that the shoulder is locked...
Good...
As if your arm were made of one solid piece of wood...
And feel that feeling that your arm is rigid and solid as if it were made out of a piece of wood...

You can actually feel it locking into position...

It is so solid so rigid that if I push down it simply bounces back up...

It is completely locked in place...

It is so solid so rigid that if I push up it simply bounces back down...

It is completely locked in place..."

Push the arm to test

"Good completely rigid...

So rigid so tightly locked in place that...

Completely stiff and rigid like a block of wood...

In a moment I'm going to count from one to three...

And when I do I want you to try to lower your arm...

You will try to lower your arm but it will not move...

Because it is so rigid so completely rigid it will not move...

The harder you try to move it the harder it is...

One...

The harder you try the harder it is...

Two...

You cannot move your arm...

Three...

The harder you try the harder it is...

The harder you try the stiffer it becomes...

You cannot move your arm....

Good now stop trying...

In a moment I am going to touch your arm...

As soon as I touch your arm it will return to normal...

Take their arm at the wrist and elbow

Good your arm feels quite normal...

All feelings of stiffness completely disappeared...

Your arm is now becoming completely limp and relaxed...

(Lower their arm back down onto their leg whilst saying)

And as your arm goes completely limp and relaxed...

You feel yourself becoming more deeply relaxed...

Going deeper and deeper and deeper...

And the deeper you go the better you feel...

The better you feel the deeper you go."

You can now be sure that a light trance has been achieved. Carry on with another test/ convincer/deepener to medium stage.

"In a moment...

Not yet...

When I say...

I'm going to ask you to count from one to ten...

When you count from one up to ten you will find that...

The number seven has completely disappeared from your memory...

But you will have forgotten to remember the number seven...

The number seven is completely disappearing for you now...

That number is gone....gone....gone.....

When I say I want you to count slowly...

One...

Two...

Three...

Four...

Five...

Six...

Eight...

Nine...

Ten...

Nod your head when you understand...

Wait for the nod.

Now count slowly from one to ten...."

They count up from one to ten leaving out the number seven they may even pause slightly and appear to struggle.

"Good...

Now once again count up from one to ten...

And one more time...

Count nice and s..l..o..w..l..y...

From one up to ten...

Good well done...

And relax...

In a moment I'm going to wake you and when you are awake you will find...

That even though your eyes are open....you continue to count in this way...

Forgetting the number seven...

Until I click my fingers and say SEVEN...

When I click my fingers and say SEVEN...

You will remember the number seven...

Nod your head when you understand....

One...

Two...

Three...

Open your eyes...

Good...

Can you count from one to ten out loud for me?..."

They count and miss out seven. This will usually bring about a confused or amused reaction, sometimes a bit of both. You then continue. Click your fingers and say SEVEN.

"Now can you count out loud for me from one to ten..."

They count properly not missing any numbers.

"Good now SLEEP...

And relax...

Now the number seven has returned...

For you...

It's back where it belongs...

Everything returning to normal..."

The subject has now reached the medium trance station. Carry on with another test/ convincer/ deepener.

"Good...

In a moment not yet I am going to ask you to open your eyes...

When you do...

You will notice that I am holding a glass in my left hand...

In the glass is a clear liquid.....

As I count from one to five....

You will notice the colour of the liquid changing...

When I reach the number five .....

It will be as if the liquid has completely changed its colour to red...

Nod your head when you understand..."

Wait for the nod

"Good

Open your eyes and look at the glass in my hand...

One ...

Keep looking at the glass...

Because two as you keep looking...

You can see the change happening...

Three darker and darker...

Four changing colour completely...

And five...

What colour is the liquid in the glass..."

When they say red they have entered the deep stage of hypnosis. Carry on with a further test/ convincer/ deepener.

"Well done...

Now close your eyes...

And allow yourself to go ten times more deeply relaxed....

And as you become so comfortable and secure deeper and deeper with each breath you take...

And with every sound you hear....deeper...deeper...d..e..e..p..e..r...

In moment...

Not quite yet...

But shortly...

You are going to open your eyes...

On the count of three you will open your eyes...

And when you do you will notice that you cannot see the glass of water on the table...

It is as if it is invisible...

The glass of water has become completely invisible to you...

Nod your head when you understand..."

Wait for the nod.

"One...

Two...

Three...

Open your eyes wide awake...

Tell me what you see on the table..."

If they name everything but the glass then the subject has now reached hyper trance. Continue to ego strengthening, script or a combination of both.

Complete Compliance

As mentioned before we do not really use depth tests on stage or street. Instead we would use complete compliance statement after some deepeners.

"Whatever suggestion I make to you for the rest of the evening...

While we are in this room...

Will become your immediate and complete reality instantly......

Whatever I say you can see...

You will see...

What I suggest you can hear...

You can hear...

Whatever I say you can feel...

You will feel...

Whatever I suggest will be your reality...

No matter how ridiculous it might at first sound...

Nod your head when you understand..."

CHAPTER ~ 7 ~ SCRIPTS & SKETCHES

What are they

Scripts and sketches are the names we give to that which we do once a subject is hypnotised. They are the suggestions we give during hypnosis. The difference between the two is that we use a suggestion in therapy to make a permanent change for the better, and on stage to make a temporary change. Post hypnotic suggestions given during therapy are generally left active after termination as opposed to those given in stage and street which must be removed before trance termination.

Scripts

A script is pre written or memorised set of suggestions commonly used in therapy for the treatment of phobias, fears bad habits in fact just about anything. For example, a phobia is an anxious irrational reaction to something, such as fear of spiders or heights etc. As for bad habits take your pick smoking, nail biting. Let's not forget inductions these too can be scripted and often are.

In the therapy setting we would use suggestions to test for depth and also to make the changes which the subject requests, we would then use post hypnotic suggestion to reinforce the suggestion.

Sketches

Are usually comedy routines used on stage and on the street. They will be any comedic act which is suggested and then acted upon or performed by the subject whilst hypnotised.

As you can see sketches or scripts are the suggestions we make to the subject during hypnosis, once a subject is deeply hypnotised enough. There are hypnotic and post hypnotic. As with most things in hypnosis they do exactly what they say. The hypnotic suggestion is given and acted upon during trance. Whereas the post hypnotic suggestion is given during trance and acted upon after the trance is terminated.

On stage post hypnotic suggestion should be used judiciously especially when new to hypnosis. Imagine forgetting to remove a post hypnotic suggestion and a subject acting it out after they have left the venue! Health and safety anyone!

Scripts and sketches should be considered the purpose of using hypnosis, otherwise you are putting someone in a trance for no reason at all.

Post hypnotic suggestions

A post hypnotic suggestion is a suggestion made whilst a subject is under hypnosis which is to be carried out once the subject is awake. Post hypnotics can be carried out at any time in the near or even distant future.

One should always be careful to make post hypnotic suggestions very specific since they will be carried out faithfully by the subject. Always remember the health and safety of the subject! Post hypnotics are used for different reasons as we see below.

Therapy

Used to change a habit, and then to reinforce that change. It would be pointless to spend an hour or so helping your subject to become a non smoker if it only lasted for the duration of the therapy.

Stage

On stage post hypnotics can be used to add variety to the performance. Giving post hypnotic suggestions could be given to entertain the audience during an intermission is a popular part of many shows.

NOTE: for both therapy and stage post hypnotics are used to make future hypnosis quicker. Re-induction suggestions are given during the trance termination sequence as a rule, the suggestion can use any trigger you prefer. You may say something like

"Whenever I click my fingers you will return to this wonderful relaxed trance"

In street hypnotism post hypnotics are used widely to give the illusion of magic powers.

Sample post hypnotic suggestions

Therapy

"I am now going to give you a post hypnotic suggestion...

This type of suggestion is the most powerful...

Because it is implanted deep...

So very deep...

In your subconscious...

From now on every time you see the colour red...

Each and every time...

You see red...

It could be in a painting...

Or the colour of a car...

A light...

Every time you come across red...

Will serve as a sign to your subconscious mind...

That you are a...

Non smoker...

Reinforcing the good work we have done here today...

Each and every time you see red...

Helps to motivate you to continue a healthy...

Lifestyle...

Confident that the decision to be smoke free...

Is the right choice...

For you..."

Continue to the termination

Stage

"All the time you are in this theatre...

Whenever you hear me say...

Behind you...

You will stand...

And shout at the top of your voice...

Oh no he isn't...

Every time I say behind you...

You will feel compelled to stand and shout oh no he's not...

Then sit back down as if nothing had happened...

You will only do this whilst in this theatre and attending this show...

Or until I tell you otherwise...

Nod your head when you understand."

Continue on with your other subjects.

CHAPTER ~ 8 ~ AWAKENINGS

This is the end

The awakening, emergence or termination is the process of actually terminating trance completely. If you have used fractioning during the hypnosis the subject may have appeared many times to have been 'awake' however these waking states are in fact falsehoods. The subject must still be brought back fully to the land of the living. They must have all superfluous suggestions removed and be checked for normality!

The timbre of the awakening should be upbeat. Remember the purpose is to bring the subject out of trance so the voice should be used in such a way as to encourage this. No more the slow soothing tones of progressive relaxation. We may start quite slowly and soothing however we should increase in the level of urgency and volume. In the case of the stage and street there may be no perceptible change in the use of voice but in therapy it should be noticeable.

Sample awakenings

Therapy

"In a moment I am going to count from one to ten...

After which you will fully awaken...

As I count from one through to ten...

You will feel yourself...

Gradually waking up...

From this trance state...

Feeling wonderful...

Feeling as though you have had a five hour massage and a good eight hour sleep...

One.....

Two.....

Three.....

Starting to come back to the room...

Beginning to feel the chair beneath you...

Four.....

And at any time in the future...

Whenever you chose to do more work with hypnosis...

All I will have to do is click my fingers like this...

And you can return back to this wonderfully relaxed state...

In fact it will be as if...

You will have gone ten times more deeply relaxed...

Five.....

Knowing that you have the confidence to achieve any goal...

Knowing that the positive changes you have made...

Here today...

Will last...

Six.....

For ever...

Knowing that seeing red only serves a signal of strength and confidence...

That you will live smoke free...

Seven...

Remembering to forget whilst you forget to remember...

Eight...

Now feeling the chair beneath you and becoming aware of your surroundings...

Nine...

Feeling more and more alert...

Feeling refreshed and fit and ready to face the rest of your day....

Ten...

And in your own time...

Open your eyes and come fully back into the room."

Stage

"In a moment I am going to count from one to five...

At which time you will be fully awake...

Refreshed full of beans ready to continue the rest of your day...

Feeling wonderful...

As if you have had a five hour massage and an eight hour sleep.....

You will be completely normal in every way...

One...

Starting to become more alert....

Two..

Returning to normal...

And all suggestions given to you now gone completely....

Three....

Feeling more and more awake and aware..

Four...

Eyes starting to open....

And Five...

Eyes open wide awake."

Street

"Now I want you to slowly and in your own time...

Just allow yourself to come back to the here and now...

Fully alert and content...

In your own time...

That's it...

And there...

WIDE AWAKE!"

CHAPTER ~ 9 ~ RECORDINGS

Record Everything!

We can make video and audio recordings of actual inductions sketches and therapy. There is also the stock type recordings used for background and self help etc. Just to remind you one more time Record Everything!

As a legal defence.

Making video recording of your sessions gives unequivocal visual evidence of what actually happened. In the new world of constant litigation and no win no fee parasites video records are an excellent tool. The camera does not lie. Record everything from introduction to the final farewell. Give no room for ambiguity.

As background

Recordings can be used to aid the induction process. Either soothing music, subliminal messages or indeed a combination of both. These can be invaluable either in the therapy room or on stage. On stage you can also have recordings of music for both background and as triggers for your comedy sketches.

As substitute to repeating

Recordings of therapy scripts can be used to avoid repetition for the therapist. Although not a favourite of mine, many therapists once the preliminaries are over with will switch on a recording of an induction to save themselves having to repeat themselves over and over again. Also useful if the hypnotist themselves are particularly susceptible to 'nodding off' whilst performing inductions. This phenomenon is more common than you might think.

Post therapy reinforcing.

Again for therapeutic uses a recording can be used for self help especially after actual hypnotic therapy session with yourself. Reinforcing the message with a tailored recording can work wonders for the subject. I myself have read literature, by hypnotists using older less reliable methods, where they insist the subject should use a recording made by the hypnotist for several weeks after the live session in order to help with phobias etc.

General sales

For sale to the general public for either self help or entertainment. Making self help audio recordings can be a good source of income. Make simple recordings with generic inductions, scripts and emergence. These can be sold to anyone from your website, after a show or therapy session.

When making these over the counter type of recording always remember to insert disclaimers and health and safety advice. Such as informing the user not to drive or use machinery whilst listening. To make sure they are comfortable and safe. Not to listen to the recording if they are using drugs or alcohol.

Always tell them that if their urgent attention is needed in the here and now that they will awaken immediately and be out of trance.

Of course recordings of shows are always in demand especially directly after a show.

CHAPTER ~ 10 ~ PUTTING IT ALL TOGETHER

Therapy

"Hypnosis is a kind of altered state of consciousness, Your subconscious becomes very open to suggestion, when you are in this state you can make positive changes to just about anything in your life. Most people who have experienced it say that it is like daydreaming and that it is very pleasant. You are aware of everything that goes on at no time are you out of control. I am only here as a sort of guide to help you to hypnotise yourself because all hypnosis is self hypnosis.

In fact just about everyone is hypnotisable some people go very deep and others not so some take quite a bit of time and others achieve it very quickly. As I have mentioned it is just a sort of daydream state and we all daydream, sometimes we daydream several times a day. In hypnosis we just sort of extend the time of the daydream to suit us

You cannot be made to do things that you don't want to do.

You may have seen a stage show on TV or even live and thought that the people on stage lose control that the hypnotist has some power over them. Those people have volunteered themselves and are game for a laugh but could stop anytime they really wanted. You retain your basic morals and beliefs and if I made a suggestion that was to conflict with those you would simply wake up. So you can't be made to hurt yourself or anyone.

You cannot be made to divulge secrets, in fact it is why hypnotism is not used as a reliable source for a confession in court.

Another thing that some people may think is that you can get stuck in trance. Well you cannot get stuck in hypnosis, You do not go into a deep sleep like the princess in the fairy tale. In fact if I use the word sleep it just refers to that daydream state where your eyes are closed and your body and mind are completely relaxed.

Are there any other things you'd like to know about hypnosis?

Describe to me what it is that you have come here for today.

Good and so we can help with that.

Do you have any further questions?

Good and are you ok to do the hypnosis now. Good let's begin.

Hold your hands out in front of you clasp your hands together

and interlock your fingers except your index fingers. Point your index fingers out straight away from you and keep them about an inch apart.

Focus all your concentration directly at the space in between your fingers...

And notice how the two fingers are being attracted towards each other...

Allow yourself to imagine that your fingers are like powerful magnets being attracted to each other...

Don't force it just let it happen...

I don't know if it will happen immediately or if it will take a minute...

Whatever is right for you...

And as I talk to you and you concentrate...

You find that those fingers are getting closer and closer together...

The gap between those fingers getting smaller and smaller...

There notice how much closer they are getting...

It's just as if those fingers are being magnetically pulled towards each other...

Closer...closer...and closer.

Moving comfortably closer together all the time...

There now they are touching...

Did you think that would work for you?

That's the power of your mind. How amazing is that?

Look at me...

I want you to put your hands straight out in front of you and lock your elbows.

Now place your palms together and interlock your fingers like so.

Now look at those hands and use all of your imagination and concentration...

Squeeze the palms of your hands together as hard as you can.

And press your fingers into the backs of your hands as hard as you can too....

Now whilst you are pressing firmly I want you to imagine that the worlds strongest superglue is between your palms bonding your hands together....

At the same time that same superglue is on your fingers and is starting to stick your fingers to the back of your hands...

As I speak I want you to now start to imagine your fingers and your hands are becoming stuck together...

The glue is so strong a fast acting your hands are becoming stuck together...

Becoming so tightly stuck together it's as if your hands and fingers are made from one piece of material....

As if they were like one piece of solid wood....

As you imagine that piece of solid wood...

I want you feel your hands becoming more and more stuck together....

In fact they are so tightly stuck together...

That if you were to try to pull them apart you would find it impossible....

In fact they are so tightly stuck together so solid...

That when you try to pull them apart they simply stick even tighter....

The harder you try the harder it is...

The harder you try the harder it is...

When I count from one to three they will be so tightly stuck together that the harder you try to separate them the harder it becomes the more stuck they are....

ONE...sticking tighter and tighter....

TWO...hands stuck tightly together....

THREE...completely stuck....

The harder you try to pull them apart the more stuck they become....

You cannot pull them apart!

Try but you cannot pull them apart you cannot pull them apart!!

Stop trying now....

Now your arms your fingers and hands become unglued...

Pull them apart as they are now quite normal again...

Make yourself as comfortable as you can...

Take a really deep breath...

Take another really deep breath and hold it for five seconds...

Now take one last deep breath and hold it again for five seconds and as you breathe out just allow your eyes to close....

And relax...

And as you allow your eyes to relax I want you to concentrate on those eyes...

Allow your full attention to focus on your eyes and in particular the eyelids...

And the tiny muscles that control the eyelids...

Yes all those tiny muscles all around the eyes and eyelids...

Those tiny muscles that when they tense and tighten cause your eyelids to open...

Think of those muscles and think of relaxing those muscles...

Relax those muscles so much that they won't open...

Keep concentrating all those tiny muscles and how comfortably relaxed you can make them.....

Good now I want you to Imagine what it will be like if your eyelids were so relaxed that they won't open...

Really focus on imagining what that sensation would be like...

That sensation of your eyelids being so completely so comfortably relaxed that they just won't work...

And when you know that you have relaxed the muscles around those eyes and eyelids...

When you are certain that they are so relaxed that they will not open you can go ahead and try...

When you know they are so relaxed they will not work...

Not until you are absolutely sure that they won't work...

And once you are sure that they won't work you can try to open them...

That's right you can try to open them but the harder you try the more they just want to stay closed...

The harder you try the harder it becomes to open them.

That's it when you're ready try...

Try to open your eyes it is impossible...

Stop trying...

And now as I count to three your eyes and eyelids return to normal.

One ...two...three....

Put your arms out straight in front of you.

Have the palm of your right hand facing down toward the ground.

With the palm of your left hand, facing upwards toward the ceiling, like this.

In a moment...not yet...when I tell you I want you to take three deep breaths.

And as you exhale on the third breath I'm going to get you to close your eyes..

Imagine that tied to your left hand is a Piece of string...

On the other end of the piece of string is a large red balloon...

Full of helium...

At the same time Imagine that in your left hand is a stack of library books...

Very heavy old library books...

And as those heavy library books begin to weigh down on your left hand...

So the red balloon starts to pull your right hand up...

Feel it rising slowly into the air...

Good as you can feel me place more books in your left hand...

And your left hand begins to go down and down...

Your right hand and arm rising all the time...

Because your left hand and arm are moving down...

More and more...

Left hand down...

Right arm up...

Now open your eyes.

Stand with your feet together. And your hands down by your side.

Take a deep breath and hold it for a second...

Good let it go...

Take another deep breath and hold it again...

And let go...

And one more time a really deep breath...

Hold...

And let it go...

Good as I stand behind you I want you to imagine...

That there is a magnetic force building up...

A force that is pulling you backwards...

Feel it pulling you further and further...

Just allow it to happen...

Don't worry I won't let you fall...

Just allow yourself...

Feel yourself being pulled back more and more...

Pick a point on the ceiling and look up at that point...

do not take your eyes off it for a moment...

As you sit there looking at the ceiling I want you to become aware of your body...

In a moment I'm going to get you to take three deep breaths. Not yet...

In a moment...

I'm going to get you to breath in as deeply as you can through your nose...

Then I want you to hold your breath while I count to three...

Then I want you to breath out through your mouth gently and slowly. Do you understand?

OK keeping your eyes firmly fixed on that point on the ceiling...

Take a nice deep breath in...

Now hold it...1...2...3

And exhale...

And again take a nice deep breath in...

Hold it...1...2...3

And exhale...

And one more time...

Breathe in...

Hold it...1...2...3

And exhale...

Good...

You probably already noticed that you feel a bit more relaxed generally...

Because whenever we breath out our body tends to relax a little bit...

It's just that we are not usually aware of it...

In a moment I'm going to ask you to do this breathing exercise three more times...

And this time each time you breath...

Out I want you to notice that feeling of relaxation on each out breath...

Good take a nice deep breath in...

And hold it...1...2...3

And slowly exhale feeling that wave of relaxation as the air passes across your lips...

Feel your whole body relax...

That's it good...

And again take a really deep breath all the way down...

Hold it..1...2...3

And exhale...

And as you exhale feel yourself becoming more relaxed...

And one last time...

Breath in slowly through your nose deeper and deeper...

And hold...1...2...3

And breath out slowly releasing any remaining tension...

Now that you are completely relaxed...

I want you to think about your toes and as you think about your toes...

Imagine they are becoming more relaxed as if they were twice as relaxed...

Feel any tension just melt away...

And take that feeling of relaxation and allow it to move up through your feet...

Feel the deep relaxation in every part of your feet top and bottom...

Good...

I want you now to let that feeling spread up through from your toes and feet...

All the way up through your shins and calves right up to your knees...

As you feel that relaxation allow it to spread further up through the tops of your legs all the way to your waist...

So from your toes right up to your waist is completely relaxed...

Now take that relaxation and feel it spread further up through your chest and back...

And along your shoulders and arms too...

Feel that pleasant wonderful feeling of relaxation...

Right from your toes through your entire body up to your neck...

Enjoy this feeling and allow it to move from your neck...

And around your head all the way around the back of your head...

And at the same time up across your face...

And all the way to your eyes...

Feel now all the muscles around your eyes relaxing...

And as they relax...

You feel your eyes becoming...

Heavier...

Heavier and heavier as all the tiny muscles let go of any remaining tension...

And the eye lids just close...

I want you to imagine you are standing at the top of a staircase on a landing...

You look down and see that the staircase itself is very well lit...

You look to the side a see a very sturdy hand rail...

See yourself reaching out and putting your hand on the rail...

That's right and you feel just how strong the rail is...

In a moment I am going to count from ten down to one...

And as I count down I want you to walk down the steps...

One at a time with each number...

And with each number you will become more relaxed...

Ten step onto the first step and as you do feel that feeling of moving down...

And nine going down onto the next step...

And when you step onto that step feel yourself relaxing becoming more comfortable...

Eight going down feeling more relaxed...

Seven...

As if you meant to go twice as deeply relaxed...

Six...

Down onto the next step and because five takes you even further into relaxation...

It's as if with each step you become twice as deeply relaxed twice as comfortable be...four...

You go down deeper and deeper and...

Three just makes you feel so relaxed two be more relaxed than you have ever felt..

And down now...

Right down to the bottom and one...

Completely at ease...

Completely relaxed

In a moment I'm going to lift up your arm in front of you...

Now imagine that the elbow is locked...

And now that the shoulder is locked...

Good...

As if your arm were made of one solid piece of wood...

And feel that feeling that your arm is rigid and solid as if it were made out of a piece of wood...

You can actually feel it locking into position...

It is so solid so rigid that if I push it simply bounces back...

It is completely locked in place...

Good completely rigid...

So rigid so tightly locked in place that..

Completely stiff and rigid like a block of wood...

In a moment I'm going to count from one to three...

And when I do I want you to try to lower your arm...

You will try to lower your arm but it will not move...

Because it is so rigid so completely rigid it will not move...

The harder you try to move it the harder it is...

One...

The harder you try the harder it is...

Two...

You cannot move your arm...

Three...

The harder you try the harder it is...

The harder you try the stiffer it becomes...

You cannot move your arm...

Good....

Now stop trying...

In a moment I am going to touch your arm...

As soon as I touch your arm it will return to normal...

Good your arm feels quite normal...

All feelings of stiffness completely disappeared...

Your arm is now becoming completely limp and relaxed...

And as your arm goes completely limp and relaxed...

And as it drops back onto your leg...

You feel yourself becoming ten times more deeply relaxed...

Going deeper and deeper and deeper...

In a moment...

Not yet..

When I say...

I will ask you to count from one to ten...

When you count from one up to ten you will find that..

The number seven has completely disappeared from your memory...

You will not remember the number seven...

The number seven is completely disappearing for you now...

That number is gone...

Gone..

Gone.....

When I say in a MOMENT...

I want you to count slowly...

One...two...three...four...five...six...eight...nine...ten...

Nod your head when you understand...

Now count slowly from one to ten....

Good...

Now once again count up from one to ten...

And one more time...

Count nice and s.lo.w.l.y.

From one up to ten...

Good well done...

And relax...

In a moment I'm going to wake you and when you are awake you will find...

That even though your eyes are open...

You continue to count in this way...

Forgetting the number seven...

Until I click my fingers and say SEVEN...

When I click my fingers and say SEVEN...

You will remember the number seven...

Nod your head when you understand...

One...two...three...open your eyes...

Good...

Can you count from one to ten out loud for me...

Good well done...

Seven...

Now can you count out loud for me from one to ten...

Good now SLEEP....

Good...

And relax...

Now the number seven has returned...

For you..

It's back where it belongs...

Everything returning to normal...."

...INSERT THERAPY SCRIPT HERE...

"In a moment I am going to count from one to ten...

After which you will fully awaken...

As I count from one through to ten...

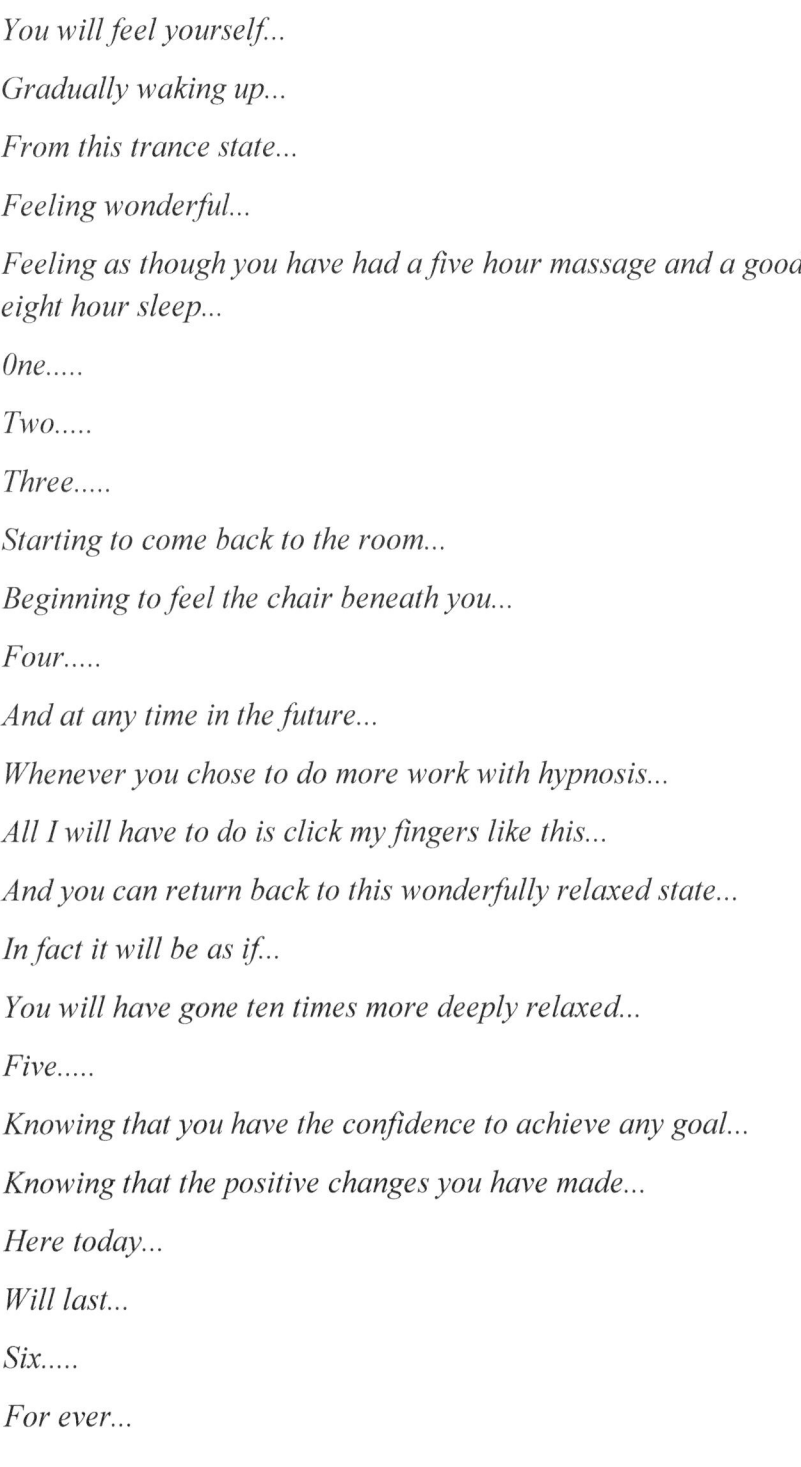

You will feel yourself...

Gradually waking up...

From this trance state...

Feeling wonderful...

Feeling as though you have had a five hour massage and a good eight hour sleep...

One.....

Two.....

Three.....

Starting to come back to the room...

Beginning to feel the chair beneath you...

Four.....

And at any time in the future...

Whenever you chose to do more work with hypnosis...

All I will have to do is click my fingers like this...

And you can return back to this wonderfully relaxed state...

In fact it will be as if...

You will have gone ten times more deeply relaxed...

Five.....

Knowing that you have the confidence to achieve any goal...

Knowing that the positive changes you have made...

Here today...

Will last...

Six.....

For ever...

Knowing that seeing red only serves a signal of strength and confidence...

That you will live smoke free...

Seven...

Remembering to forget whilst you forget to remember...

Eight...

Now feeling the chair beneath you and becoming aware of your surroundings...

Nine...

Feeling more and more alert...

Feeling refreshed and fit and ready to face the rest of your day....

Ten...

And in your own time...

Open your eyes and come fully back into the room."

Stage

"*Good evening everyone my name is Steve Leap...*

Tonight be prepared to be amazed not by me because I am not the star of the show. No tonight ladies and gentlemen you are the stars of the show.

Soon I will be asking for volunteers to join me on stage. Even those of you who do not volunteer beware because now that you have heard my voice and seen my eyes you may go into trance at anytime.

To be hypnotised is very simple in fact many experts believe that all hypnosis is merely self hypnosis. To be hypnotised you need to be capable of four things. ICIF a good IMAGINATION....Good powers of CONCENTRATION... reasonable INTELLIGENCE... and be able to FOLLOW instructions.

There are a few people I am not allowed to hypnotise those are people who are drunk, people with mental health issues, or serious health issues of any kind, pregnant women, and anyone high on drugs and anyone under the age of eighteen. Anyone falling into any of the above categories should not volunteer.

Hypnosis is a quite natural state whereby a person in trance is highly suggestible and that just about anything is possible. No one will be taking their clothes this is a family show.

So please volunteers this way!

Everyone look at me. I want you to put your hands out in front of you and lock your elbows. Now place your palms together and interlock your fingers like so.

Now look at your hands and use all of your imagination and concentration...

Squeeze the palms of your hands together as hard as you can and press your fingers into the backs of your hands as hard as you can too...

Now whilst you are pressing firmly I want you to imagine that there is the strongest superglue known to man between your palms bonding your hands together....

At the same time that same superglue is on your fingers and is starting to stick your fingers to the back of your hands...

As I speak I want you to now start to imagine your fingers and your hands are becoming stuck together...

Becoming so tightly stuck together it's as if your hands and fingers are made from one piece of material...

As if they were like one piece of solid wood...

As you imagine that piece of solid wood I want you feel your hands becoming more and more stuck together...

In fact they are so tightly stuck together that if you were to try to pull them apart you would find it impossible...

In fact they have become so tightly stuck together so solid that when you try to pull them apart they simply stick even tighter...

When I count from one to three they will be so tightly stuck together that the harder you try to separate them the harder it becomes the more stuck they are....

ONE...sticking tighter and tighter....

TWO...hands stuck tightly together....

THREE...completely stuck....

The harder you try to pull them apart the more stuck they become....

You cannot pull them apart! Try but you cannot pull them apart you cannot pull them apart!!

Stop trying now....

Make yourself as comfortable as you can...

Now close your eyes...

Take that stuck...

That superglue feeling...

And allow it to spread into your eyelids...

And notice how not only your hands are stuck...

But now the eyes are stuck shut too...

The harder you try to open them...

The tighter they stick...

On the count of three your eyes will return to normal

One...

Two...

Three...

Open your eyes...

Look at your hand...

In particular focus on the differences in the skin tone...

Because as you notice the various subtle variations...

You begin to notice other things...

Like the number of lines in the skin....

And you can focus on one of those lines...

And as you focus on that line...

You begin to notice that your hand is starting to move down...

Away from your face...

And as that happens....

In your own time....

Because as your hand slowly drops...

So you feel your eyes closing....

As if the eyelids were just too...

Heavy to stay open...

As if they were just too relaxed to bother to stay open ...

And as they close you feel yourself relax completely...

And sleep...

That's right you have used your excellent powers of intelligence, concentration and imagination...

To become relaxed I want you to concentrate a bit more...

I'm going to count from 10 down to 1 and as I count I want you to Picture the number in your minds eye...

As I say each number in turn picture it...

And when I say gone let the number disappear...

And as you do let that number disappear...

You become even more relaxed...

NOD YOUR HEADS WHEN YOU UNDERSTAND...

10...

Picture the number 10...

And gone...

Relax...

9.....

And gone.....

8.......

Gone and allow yourself to continue relax every single muscle in your body....

7....

And gone.....

6...

Still relaxing as the number is gone......

5.....

Gone......

4.......

Gone.....

3 and because it's gone it just serves to take you so deep....

2.....

Gone...

And 1.....

Gone down to every fibre and of your being....

Every muscle completely relaxed.....

And the deeper you relax the better you feel...

While the better you feel the deeper you relax

And from now on every word that I say...

Every sound you hear just serves to take you deeper....

Especially laughter and applause....

Each time you hear laughter or applause it's as if you go twice as deep as before...

Please give everyone on stage a huge round of applause!

As they just continue to go deeper and deeper."

...SKETCHES GO HERE...

"In a moment I am going to count from one to five...

At which time you will be fully awake...

Refreshed full of beans ready to continue the rest of your day...

Feeling wonderful...

As if you have had a five hour massage and an eight hour sleep.....

You will be completely normal in every way...

One...

Starting to become more alert....

Two..

Returning to normal...

And all suggestions given to you gone completely...

Three....

Feeling more and more awake and aware..

Four...

Eyes starting to open....

And Five...

Eyes open wide awake."

Street

"Well it's nothing more than a sort of guided meditation really. Everybody does it all the time like daydreaming. Have you ever driven your car somewhere on say a regular journey and when you arrive you think to yourself how the heck did I get here?

Well that's a very light form of hypnosis. Your subconscious mind has driven you home and your conscious mind has been doing the important things in the here and now, like wondering what's for dinner or what's on the TV later. The only difference is that when you get hypnotised by a professional like myself is that you get expert guidance to make the very most of the experience. In fact people have told me the feeling they get when hypnotised is so good it's like the second best feeling they've ever had.

Well I can show you a couple of tricks if you like.

Just want to make sure you're not pregnant, or on any kind of drugs, legal or otherwise, and that you are over eighteen.

Stand up straight take a deep breath. I am going to stand behind you. I want you to just let whatever happens happen. I'm not sure what will happen but when it does don't worry I won't let you fall. I'll be back here to catch you. OK?
I want you to look at your left foot...

let me come around to that side...

OK focus on that foot ...

Really look at it...

And as you look at it...

I want you to use your imagination...

I know you have a fantastic imagination from the exercise we just did...

So really focus down and imagine that you have just stepped on a tube of the strongest...

Fastest acting glue in the world...

And as you look you can actually feel that glue taking effect...

It's starting to bond the bottom of your shoe...

To the floor...

You can actually feel your foot becoming stuck...

To...

The...

Floor...

Sticking tighter and tighter...

The more you look the more stuck it becomes...

The glue is so strong that if you try to lift your foot...

It won't budge...

In fact the harder you try to lift it...

The harder it is...

The harder you try the more stuck it becomes...

Try and you cannot...

Try and you cannot lift your foot...

Stop trying!

Just as your foot is stuck to the floor you find that...

When I take your hand and put it here...

It too will be stuck...

Look it's stuck...

I can move take it off...

But when I place it back on your head...

It immediately becomes stuck just as strongly stuck as your foot is to the floor...

Now I am going to count to three...

And as soon as I reach three your hand will become normal again and you can put it down.....one....two...three...hand back to normal.

And as I count to three again your foot will return completely to normal and you will be able to move it...

One...

Two...

Three...

Foot back to normal...

Right sit down and close your eyes...

And as soon as your eyes are closed they will become tightly stuck together...

Just as your foot stuck to the floor...

And your hand stuck to your head...

Your eyes are now closed and will not open...

Try and open them and they will not..

The harder you try the tighter they become...

Stop trying and sleep.

I'm going to lift your arm and hold it out in front of you...

As soon as I let go you will find it is stuck there...

You cannot move it...

The harder you try the more rigid it becomes...

If I tap it...

It will just bounce back...

There you see...

If I take hold of your arm it will move for me...

But as soon as I let go it locks into place exactly where I let go of it..."

...SKETCHES HERE...

"Now I want you to slowly and in your own time...

Just allow yourself to come back to the here and now...

Fully alert and content...

In your own time...

That's it...

And there...

WIDE AWAKE!"

CHAPTER ~ 11 ~ APPENDIX

Training/ Certification

Training is an important part of learning and honing any skill there are different ways to learn as discussed below. Learning or improving any skill depends on the individual since we all learn in different ways. You should use the style or combination of styles which suits you best. Beware price is not necessarily a good indicator of quality.

Distance learning

Distance learning courses are available absolutely everywhere. Spend just ten minutes on the web and you will find dozens of distance learning courses available. There are no hard and fast rules for choosing the best for you. The best indicator of how good, or bad, a course may be is genuine feedback from past students. Beware, look for truly independent evaluations.

So the pros and cons. The pros are that you can learn at your own pace reading re-reading and practicing without the pressure if you have a busy life this kind of learning is perfect. Most of these courses offer some kind of support usually online which can be invaluable.

Books

Reading books is another option. The upside of reading all the books you can get your hands on is that you will get many points of view with regard to every single aspect of hypnotism. You can also see the parts which suit or don't suit, whichever the case may be, you as an individual.

CD's/ DVD's

Listening to CD's and watching DVD's is a common way for anyone to learn. The advantages are that you can actually hear and/or see the process taking place and therefore mimic to a certain degree what others are doing. Watch these videos very closely for the little things that the hypnotists do as well as the larger overt things.

Live Course

All of the above are feasible ways to learn the basics of hypnotism. You cannot however do better than a live course given by a competent instructor. The benefits are that you can gain valuable insights, hints and tips from the instructors own experience. Questions can be asked and answered directly and of course you can practice and have honest feedback helping you to hone your skills.

Regardless of the root you choose to take to educate yourself it is very important to remember that there are no legally recognised qualifications. Any certificate issued will only ever be recognised by the issuing organisation. Certain qualifications may be required in order to practice therapy under the auspices of a named society or association and may also be required in order to secure insurance.

The Law

The Hypnotism Act 1952.

An Act to regulate the demonstration of hypnotic phenomena for the purpose of public entertainment.

In short the Act states that you must have a license granted by the local authority to perform hypnotism for entertainment purposes in public.

This refers specifically to places where the public attend and expect to be entertained. Also any licensed premises where alcohol is served. This relates to whether the public are being charged a fee or not.

You may not perform hypnosis on anyone under the age of eighteen for the purpose of entertainment in public.

However these restrictions do not apply if you are performing hypnotism for scientific research purposes or as a curative process.

So if you say you are performing experiments then the age limit does not apply neither does the need to have a license granted by a local authority.

Below you will find two versions of the hypnotism act. First the entire act and secondly a local authority interpretation of the act used as conditions for hypnotism Both of these documents are in the public domain.

Hypnotism Act 1952

1952 CHAPTER 46 15 and 16 Geo 6 and 1 Eliz 2

An Act to regulate the demonstration of hypnotic phenomena for purposes of public entertainment.

[1st August, 1952]

Annotations:

Modifications etc. (not altering text)

C1Act: functions of local authority not to be responsibility of an executive of the authority

1Control of demonstrations of hypnotism at places licensed for public entertainment.

(1)Where under any enactment an authority in any area have power to grant licences for the regulation of places kept or ordinarily used for public dancing, singing, music or other public entertainment of the like kind, any power conferred by any enactment to attach conditions to any such licence shall include power to attach conditions regulating or prohibiting the giving of an exhibition, demonstration or performance of hypnotism on any person at the place to which the licence relates.

(2)In the application of this section to Scotland, for the reference to places kept or ordinarily used for public dancing, singing, music or other public entertainment of the like kind there shall be substituted a reference to theatres or other places of public amusement or public entertainment.

2Control of demonstrations of hypnotism at other places.

(1)No person shall give an exhibition, demonstration or performance of hypnotism on any living person at or in connection with an entertainment to which the public are admitted, whether on payment or otherwise, at any place in relation to which such a licence as is mentioned in section one of this Act is not in force unless the controlling authority have authorised that exhibition, demonstration or performance.

[F1(1A)The foregoing subsection shall not apply to an exhibition, demonstration or performance of hypnotism that takes place in the course of a performance of a play (within the meaning of the Theatres Act 1968) given either at premises in respect of which a licence under that Act is in force or under the authority of any such letters patent as are mentioned in section 17(1) of that Act.]

(2)Any authorisation under this section may be made subject to any conditions.

(3)If a person gives any exhibition, demonstration or performance of hypnotism in contravention of this section, or in contravention of any conditions attached to an authorisation under this section, he shall be liable on summary conviction to a fine not exceeding [F2level 3 on the standard scale].

[F3(4)In this section, the expression "controlling authority" in relation to a place in any area means the authority having power to grant licences of the kind mentioned in section 1 above in that area.]

Annotations:

Extent Information

E1This version of this provision extends to England and Wales only; a separate version has been created for Scotland only.

Amendments (Textual)

F1S. 2(1A) inserted by Theatres Act 1968 (c. 54), **Sch. 2**

F2Words substituted by virtue of (E.W.) Criminal Justice Act 1982 (c. 48, SIF 39:1), [F1 and (S.) Criminal Procedure (Scotland) Act 1975 (c. 21, SIF 39:1) ss. 289F, 289G

F3S. 2(4) substituted (E.W.) by Local Government (Miscellaneous Provisions) Act 1982 (c. 30, SIF 81:1), s. 1, **Sch. 2 para. 1**

2Control of demonstrations of hypnotism at other places. S

(1)No person shall give an exhibition, demonstration or performance of hypnotism on any living person at or in connection with an entertainment to which the public are admitted, whether on payment or otherwise, at any place in relation to which such a licence as is mentioned in section one of this Act is not in force unless the controlling authority have authorised that exhibition, demonstration or performance.

[F7(1A)The foregoing subsection shall not apply to an exhibition, demonstration or performance of hypnotism that takes place in the course of a performance of a play (within the meaning of the Theatres Act 1968) given either at premises in respect of which a licence under that Act is in force or under the authority of any such letters patent as are mentioned in section 17(1) of that Act.]

(2)Any authorisation under this section may be made subject to any conditions.

(3)If a person gives any exhibition, demonstration or performance of hypnotism in contravention of this section, or in contravention of any conditions attached to an authorisation under this section, he shall be liable on summary conviction to a fine not exceeding [F8level 3 on the standard scale].

(4)In this section, the expression "controlling authority" means—

(a)in relation to a place in any such area as is mentioned in section one of this Act, the authority having power to grant licences of the kind mentioned in that section in that area;

(b)in relation to a place in any other area in England, the council of the . . . F9 district where the place is, and in relation to a place in any other area in Scotland, [F10[F11council constituted under section 2 of the Local Government etc. (Scotland) Act 1994] for the area] where the place is.

Annotations:

Extent Information

E2This version of this provision extends to Scotland only; a separate version has been created for England and Wales only.

Amendments (Textual)

F7S. 2(1A) inserted by Theatres Act 1968 (c. 54), **Sch. 2**

F8Words substituted by virtue of (E.W.) Criminal Justice Act 1982 (c. 48, SIF 39:1), **ss. 38**, 46 and (S.) Criminal Procedure (Scotland) Act 1975 (c. 21, SIF 39:1) ss. 289F, 289G

F9Words repealed by   Local Government Act 1972 (c. 70) , **Sch. 30**

F10 Words substituted by Local Government (Scotland) Act 1973 (c. 65), **Sch. 24 para. 40**

F11 Words in s. 2(4)(b) substituted (S.) (1.4.1996) by virtue of 1994 c. 39, s. 180(1), **Sch. 13 para. 39**; S.I. 1996/323 , **art. 4(1)(c)**

[F4 2AFee.

Annotations:

Amendments (Textual)

F4S. 2A added (21.9.1994) by 1994 c. xii, ss. 1, 7(1)

The person making an application to a controlling authority, being the council of a London borough, for an authorisation under section 2 of this Act shall on making the application pay to the council such reasonable fee as the council may determine.]

3Prohibition on hypnotising persons under twenty-one.

A person who gives an exhibition, demonstration or performance of hypnotism on a person who has not attained the age of **[F5**eighteen] years at or in connection with an entertainment to which the public are admitted, whether on payment or otherwise, shall, unless he had reasonable cause to believe that that person had attained that age, be liable on summary conviction to a fine not exceeding **[F6**level 3 on the standard scale].

Annotations:

Amendments (Textual)

F5Word substituted (S.) by Age of Majority (Scotland) Act 1969 (c. 39), s. 1(3), **Sch. 1 Pt. I** and (E.W) by Family Law Reform Act 1969 (c. 46), s. 1(3), **Sch. 1 Pt. I**

F6Words substituted by virtue of (E.W.) Criminal Justice Act 1982 (c. 48, SIF 39:1), **ss. 38**, 46 and (S.) Criminal Procedure (Scotland) Act 1975 (c. 21, SIF 39:1) ss. 289F, 289G

4Entry of premises.

Any police constable may enter any premises where any entertainment is held if he has reasonable cause to believe that any act is being or may be done in contravention of this Act.

5Saving for scientific purposes.

Nothing in this Act shall prevent the exhibition, demonstration or performance of hypnotism (otherwise than at or in connection with an entertainment) for scientific or research purposes or for the treatment of mental or physical disease.

6Interpretation.

In this Act, except where the context otherwise requires it, the following expression shall have the meaning hereby assigned to it, that is to say:—

"hypnotism" includes hypnotism, mesmerism and any similar act or process which produces or is intended to produce in any person any form of induced sleep or trance in which the susceptibility of the mind of that person to suggestion or direction is increased or intended to be increased but does not include hypnotism, mesmerism or any such similar act or process which is self-induced.

7Short title, extent and commencement.

(1)This Act may be cited as the Hypnotism Act 1952.

(2)This Act shall not extend to Northern Ireland.

(3)This Act shall come into force on the first day of April, nineteen hundred and fifty-three.

THE HYPNOTISM ACT 1952 (AS AMENDED)

CONDITIONS FOR HYPNOTISM ETC

Conditions for hypnotism, mesmerism or any similar act or process which induces or is intended to produce in any other person any form of induced sleep or trance in which the susceptibility of the mind of that person to suggestion or direction is increased or intended to be increased.

1. The council to be informed in writing 28 days in advance of the performance of

(a) the name (both real and stage, if different) and address of the person who will give
the performance (hereafter referred to as the "hypnotist), along with details of their last
three performances.(where and when); and
(b) A statement as to whether, and if so giving full details thereof, the hypnotist has
been previously refused or had withdrawn a consent by any licensing authority or been
convicted of an offence under the hypnotism act 1952 or of an offence involving the
breach of any condition regulating or prohibiting the giving of a performance of
hypnotism on any person at any theatre or other place of public amusement or public
entertainment.

2. Publicity

(a) No pester, advertisement or program for the performance which is likely to cause
public offence shall be displayed, sold or supplied by or on behalf of the licensee either
at the premises or elsewhere:

(b) Every poster, advertisement or programme for the performance, which is displayed,
sold or supplied shall include, clearly and legibility, the following statement:"Volunteers, who must be aged 18 or over, can refuse at any point to
continue taking part in the performance"

3. Insurance

(c) The performance shall be covered to a reasonable level of public liability insurance.
The hypnotist must provide the evidence of this to the local authority if requested; and
it must be available for inspection at the performance;

4. Physical arrangements

(d) the means of access between the auditorium and the stage for participants shall be
properly lit and free from obstruction;

(e) A continuous white or yellow line shall be provided on the floor of any raised stage
at a safe distance from the edge. This line shall run parallel with the edge of the stage
for its whole width. The hypnotist shall inform all subjects that they must not cross the
line while under hypnosis, unless specified to do so as part of the performance.

5. Treatment of subjects

(f) Before starting the performance the hypnotist shall make a statement to the audience, in a serious manner, identifying those groups of people who should not volunteer to participate in it; explaining what the volunteers might be asked to perform; informing the audience of the possible risks from any embarrassment or anxiety; and emphasising that the subjects may cease to participate at any time they wish. The following is a suggestion statement, which might be amended as necessary to suit individual styles as long as the overall message remains the same."I shall be looking for volunteers over 18 who are willing to be hypnotised and participate in the show. Anyone who comes forward should be prepared to take part in a range of entertaining hypnotic suggestions but can be assured that they will not be asked to do anything which is indecent, offensive or harmful. Volunteers need to be in normal physical and mental health and I must ask that no one volunteers if they have a history of mental illness, or are under the influence of alcohol or other drugs or are pregnant."

(g) No form of coercion shall be used to persuade members or the audience to participate in the performance. In particular, hypnotists shall not use selection techniques which seek to coerce onto the stage the most suggestible members of the audience without their prior knowledge of what is intended. Any use of such selection

techniques (e.g. asking members of the audience to clasp their hands together and
asking those who cannot free them again to come onto the stage) should only be used
when the audience is fully aware or what is intended and that participation is entirely
voluntary at every stage;

(h) if the volunteers are to remain hypnotised during an interval in the performance, a
reasonable number of attendants as agreed with the licensing authority shall be in
attendance throughout to ensure their safety;

6. Prohibited Actions.

(i) the performance shall be so conducted as not to be likely to cause offence to any
person in the audience or any hypnotised subject;

(j) the performance shall be so conducted as not to be likely to cause harm, anxiety or
distress to any person in the audience or any hypnotised subject. In particular, the
performance shall not include:-

(i) Any suggestion involving age regression of a subject (i.e. asking the subject to
revert to an earlier age in their life; this does not prohibit the hypnotist from asking
subjects to act as if they were a child etc);

(ii) Any suggestion that the subject has lost something (e.g. a body part) which, if it
really occurred, could cause considerable distress;

(iii) Any demonstration in which the subject is suspended between two supports (so called "catalepsy");

(iv)The consumption of any harmful or noxious substance;

(v) Any demonstration of the power of hypnosis to block pain (e.g. pushing a needle
through the skin);

(k) The performance shall not include the giving of hypnotherapy or any other form
of treatment.

7. Completion

(l) All hypnotised subject shall remain in the presence of the hypnotist and in the room
where the performance takes place until all hypnotic suggestion have been removed.

(m) All hypnotic or post hypnotic suggestion shall be completely removed from the
minds of all the subjects and the audience before the performance ends. All hypnotised
subjects shall have the suggestions removed both individually and collectively and the
hypnotists shall confirm with each of them they feel well and relaxed (the restriction
on post hypnotic suggestions does not prevent the hypnotist telling subjects that they
will feel well and relaxed after the suggestions are removed)

(n) The hypnotist shall remain available for at least 30 minutes after the show to help
deal with any problems that might arise (Such help may take the form or reassurance in
the event of headaches or giddiness but this condition does not imply that the hypnotist
is an appropriate person to treat anyone who is unwell)

Insurance

For your own protection always make sure you have good public liability insurance for either therapy or official stage performances. In this day of no win no fee anyone can have a go at you.

Organisations

There are several organisations out there associations and the like. It is entirely up to the individual which one or ones they chose to join, if any. Some insurance companies may insist you belong to an 'official' body before covering you. Although I am not keen on the idea that commercial entities can call themselves associations, it can be useful to have as many letters after your name as possible when displaying certificates etc.

Subjects well being

The subjects well being must be your first priority. Health and safety on stage is a big issue. The size of the stage and of course the 'working area' must be in suitable condition for the sketches to be carried out. Making sure there is enough distance from the edge of the stage to where the subjects are is imperative. It may be wise to put down a clearly visible line and make suggestions that no one will cross the line. Doing this a few times during the performance whilst the subjects are in trance should do the trick.

In the therapy room the wellbeing and self improvement of the subject is paramount. I would strongly suggest that anyone choosing the hypnotherapist path should also gain some counselling skills too.

CHAPTER ~ 12 ~ EXERCISESES

Now you have read and hopefully reread this book it is time to take a deep breath and have a go yourself. Instead of just parrot fashioning from the inductions and scripts etc follow the plan on the following pages. This will give you much more insight to your own skill and style and make you a much better hypnotist regardless of the path you choose to follow thereafter

Exercise one

Create your own system. Even if you take the main body of someone else's and reword it to suit yourself it's a lot better than just using someone else's that they have written to suit themselves. It will mean your material will come across more naturally:

>**Make up your own Pre-talk**

>**Make up your own Test**

>**Make up your own Induction**

>**Make up your own Deepener**

>**Make up your own ego strengthening script**

>**Make up your own therapy script/ comedy sketch**

>**Make up your own post hypnotic suggestion**

>**Make up your own awakening**

I would expect this would take most people the best part of a week depending on how fast they type etc. Read through each part several times checking for the correct terminology etc.. Once you have done this move on to the next exercise.

Exercise two

Run through your session from beginning to end several times. Use empty chairs and pillows. At first it may feel slightly awkward, but you will get used to it. This is the first time you will be able to hear yourself and practice using your voice and pacing yourself. Make plenty of notes, and change anything that does not sound or feel natural to you. Do this at least a dozen times over the next week or so. Once you are happy and comfortable move on to the next exercise.

Exercise three

Try to picture a difficult session or show & how best to handle it examples are things like someone who is overly drunk a subject having an abreaction or even a spouse or friend in the audience who may have been offended. I'm sure you can think of lots of others. Practice out loud just like an actor. Don't do this for too long a few mock-ups should do it. You are trying to achieve a level of professionalism. Hopefully you will not come across these situations too often if at all.

Exercise four

It is now time to leave the comfort of your home and get out into the big wide world. Let people know you are a hypnotist practise the susceptibility tests in public perhaps at bars or at parties. Remember the tests also constitute convincer and the introduction to inductions. Don't go for inductions yet. Just the tests, even though they may seem boring to you, certainly after doing them enough times they will, but for others they are fascinating. Try a couple of sticking feet or light heavy arms. People love these.

Exercise five.

Same as using your chairs to practice only this time use a willing volunteer and make a recording of a complete therapy session. The idea is not necessarily to do a proper session, more to see yourself in action on Video in order to critique yourself and make improvements. If you have enough volunteers try it more than once. It is amazing the things you notice in yourself. Those things which are good and equally those that are not so good and need adjusting.

Exercise six

Do either a private show or a free therapy session. This time do it for real. If you choose to do a show don't make it too long. The first time it should be under an hour. Remember you are practising and getting feedback. You will need plenty of jokes etc to keep the thing moving as well as the sketches. Remember stage is entertainment

If you choose to do a therapy session do it for free for a friend. Find someone with a nice easy phobia or habit and go for it. When you succeed in stopping a friend from smoking for instance, this is the best advertising you will ever get, word of mouth.

Exercise seven

Go to a therapist deal with any issues you may have yourself or if you feel you have no issues simply ask for ego strengthening session. More importantly observe how they carry out their session, from beginning to end. See what you can use yourself and look out for anything you may want to avoid doing.

Exercise eight

Attend a stage show. In fact you should go to these regularly. Regardless of the type of hypnosis you want to practise. Observing an ultra confident stage performer, the body language of the subjects and the material is invaluable for keeping yourself on your toes. Complacency is the worst enemy in any profession.

You may also see some bad practices, things to avoid in your own work. The fact is you can always and should always be learning something new.

AFTERWORD

I hope you have enjoyed reading this book as much as I have in attempting to write it. I am not an author and I apologise if the writing itself comes across as un polished. I am an enthusiastic amateur when it comes to writing. I am as I mention at the beginning of the book an avid student of hypnosis and all things that are associated. My hope is that you find all the above information interesting and useful. If you have then I would like to hear about it.

This book was intended to give the reader a good understanding in the groundwork required to get the complete novice started. Another book which may be of interest to you may be our 'A to Z of hypnosis a complete reference'. Designed in the style of a thesaurus it is the ideal companion to any hypnotist. With all the keywords you will come across in hypnosis. With expansive descriptions of all the important terminology as well as examples of practical uses in all the relevant areas.

If you have enjoyed this book please take the time to leave feedback. Watch out for future announcements here twitter.com/SteveLeap. Also you can contact us via e-mail at steveleapbooks@gmail.com.

Thanks again for reading.

~Disclaimer~

The author and publisher of this book have used their best efforts in the preparation of the material contained within this book. The contents of this book are for educational purposes only they do not constitute a training course in and of themselves. Should you the reader choose to implement any part of the information contained you do so at your own risk. Responsibility for implementing any of the ideas contained within are the sole responsibility of the reader.

The author and publisher make no claims as to the accuracy of the material contained within this book.